SIXTEEN
SELF SKETCHES

GEORGE BERNARD SHAW

M. Pikov del.

On Shakespear's portrait Morris ruled

Ben Jonson was by it befooled;

For who of any judgment can

Accept what is not like a man

As like the superhuman bard

Who in our calling runs me hard?

Here is my portrait for your shelf,

More like me than I'm like myself.

Not from the life did Pikov draw me

(To tell the truth he never saw me)

Yet shewed what I would have you see

Of my brief immortality.

G.B.S.

SIXTEEN SELF SKETCHES

BY BERNARD SHAW

DODD, MEAD & COMPANY · NEW YORK

Printed in the United States of America
By Quinn & Boden Company, Inc., Rahway, N. J.
Designed by Stefan Salter

CONTENTS

ILLUSTRATIONS

ILLUSTRATIONS

SIXTEEN
SELF SKETCHES

1

MY FIRST BIOGRAPHER

HE WAS MY FATHER, George Carr Shaw, writing from his office at 67 Jervis Street in the City of Dublin, where the firm of Clibborn & Shaw operated as corn merchants, not very efficiently, as Clibborn had been trained to the cloth trade, and my father to no trade at all, having been an ex-civil servant whose department in the Four Courts had been abolished and its staff pensioned. He had sold his pension, and with the capital thus procured, joined Clibborn in the business which neither of them understood, but which with offices and a warehouse in Jervis Street and a water mill in Rutland Avenue, a romantic looking village suburb of Dolphin's Barn, itself a suburb, seemed to them a promising investment. On the strength of it my father married in his middle age; and the union produced three children: the eldest Lucinda Frances (Lucy), Elinor Agnes (Aggie or Yuppy), and finally a son George Bernard (Sonny): in short, myself.

In July 1857, when I was a year old, my mother left our home in Synge Street on a visit to her father Walter Bagenal Gurly, a country gentleman of Carlow family but resident at Oughterard in Galway though for the moment his address was Kinlough in Leitrim. My mother, christened Lucinda Elizabeth Gurly (Bessie), took Lucy with her to Kinlough, leaving me and Yuppy in charge of our father.

Their correspondence begins my biography. I cannot verify it, having not the faintest recollection of learning to walk and being called Bob. However, here it is.

17th July 1857

Poor whiggedie whellow was very sick in his stomach about 1 o'clock in the night, but he is all right and as brisk as ever this morning. Nurse attributes it to some currants he ate.

20.7.

The young beggar is getting quite outrageous. I left him this morning roaring and heaving like a bull. I expect he will be able to run down the street to meet you when you are returning.

22.7.

Nurse is in great blood about having the young chap able to walk when you come back, besides I am sure she thinks it will be a great relief to herself. He made a famous attempt this morning. They were all to have gone up to your Aunt's to-day [Aunt Ellen Whitcroft].

24.7.

Bob flittered his hat to pieces yesterday and Nurse says I must give him a new one. I told her to do so herself and I will pay her, so I suppose I will be stuck. . . . Nurse says that Bob walked in great style for your Aunt.

27.7.

Nurse and Sarah [housemaid] and the two little people came over after Church and had a Royal feast in the garden. . . . Nurse got a new hat for Bob and nothing short of a Tuscan would do her so I had to hand over 10/-. However it was his birthday and so I will say nothing. . . . Yup and Bob both fell out of bed yesterday morning on the tops of their heads; neither appear to have been hurt, but they might have been.

28.7.

Bobza honors me with his company and we have walking matches together. His exploits in that way have not yet extended beyond a couple of yards which he performs in a plunge from Nurse to me and back again to Nurse or Caroline Brabazon [G. B. S.'s godmother], whoever happens to be in possession at the time being. His hat is very grand but I think Nurse will be walking into you for feathers for it when you come home.

[Undated] Sunday morning. ½ past 11 as usual.

Bob spent some time in bed with me this morning as did also breakfast etc., . . . He just got a toss but after a few roars is now laughing.

30.7.

I brought the two youngsters out yesterday morning and gave them a drive in the perambulator which they, indeed I too, enjoyed greatly. Bob is growing very unruly. The *threshing season* is approaching and he had better look out or I'll flail him.

3.8.

I will feel disappointed every morning that Bob does not stagger into me with a letter from you—and desperate fighting there is to get it from him. The young ruffian tore the newspaper this morning. Nurse and her two charges left home yesterday with the intention of spending the day at Kingstown but she happened to look in at the shop in King St and found that Miss Malone was in town which to her great disappointment put a stop to the expedition. Monday next has now been fixed for the Excursion.

6.8.

I was home in the middle of the day and had a good ½ hour's fun with Yup and Bob. . . . Cecilia [his sister, G. B. S.'s Aunt Ciss] has called to see the children.

7.8.

Nurse said to me this morning that Bob has her nearly broken down! And indeed he must be a very tiresome young-ster to mind altogether without any help.

8.8.

I delivered your kisses to Yup and Bob but contrary to your instructions I fobbed a few for myself—you know how sweet a stolen kiss is!

11.8.

Poor Bob had a narrow escape on Tuesday morning. He was sitting on the kitchen table in charge of Nurse, who merely, she says, stooped down to pick up something off the floor, when he suddenly fell back and his head went slap through a pane of glass and against the iron bar outside; miraculous to say he was not even scratched; had he fallen with his face against the glass he would have been ruined. I was in my dressing room at the time, and when I heard the crash I ran down and found Nurse so paralysed with terror that she could hardly lift the poor fellow up. I do not know how the poor fellow escaped; but it does not appear to have given him even a *pane* in his head.

15.8.

Poor Bob is annoyed with his teeth, and is consequently very uneasy both day and night.

MY FATHER AND HIS FATHER

MY MOTHER'S FATHER

2

MY APOLOGY FOR THIS BOOK

PEOPLE KEEP ASKING ME
why I do not write my own biography. I reply that I am
not at all interesting biographically. I have never killed anybody. Nothing very unusual has happened to me. The first
time I had my hands examined by a palmist he amazed me
by telling me the history of my life, or as much of it as he
had time for. Apparently he knew about things I had never
told to anyone. A few days later I mentioned in conversation
with a friend (William Archer) that I had been dabbling in
palmistry. He immediately put out his hand and challenged
me to tell him anything in his life that I did not know from
my acquaintance with him. I told him about himself exactly
what the palmist had told me about myself.

He too was amazed, just as I had been. We had believed
our experiences to be unique, whereas they were ninetynine-
point-nine per cent. the same; and of the point-one per cent.
the palmist had said nothing.

It was as if a couple of monkeys had believed their skeletons to be unique. To the extent of a bone or two they would have been right; for anatomists tell us that no two skeletons are exactly alike. Consequently a monkey is fully entitled to exhibit his unique bone or two as curiosities; but the rest of his skeleton he must reject as totally uninteresting. He must keep it to himself on pain of boring people with it intolerably.

And here comes my difficulty as an autobiographer. How am I to pick out and describe that point-five per cent. of myself that distinguishes me from other men more or less fortunate than I? What earthly interest is there in a detailed account of how the illustrious Smith was born at Number Six High Street, and grew taller and taller until he was twenty, when the obscure Brown, Jones, and Robinson, born at Number seven, eight, and nine, went through exactly the same routine of growing, feeding, excreting, dressing and undressing, lodging and moving? To justify a biography Smith must have had adventures. Exceptional things must have happened to him.

Now I have had no heroic adventures. Things have not happened to me: on the contrary it is I who have happened to them; and all my happenings have taken the form of books and plays. Read them, or spectate them; and you have my whole story: the rest is only breakfast, lunch, dinner, sleeping, wakening, and washing, my routine being just the same as everybody's routine. Voltaire tells you in two pages all you need know about Molière's private life. A hundred thousand words about it would be unbearable.

Then there is the difficulty that when an adventure does come, somebody else is usually mixed up in it. Now your right to tell your own story does not include the right to tell anyone else's. If you violate this right, and the other party still lives, you are sure to be indignantly contradicted; for no two people recollect the same incident in the same way; and very few people know what has actually happened to them, or could describe it artistically. And biographies must be artistic if they are to be readable.

The best autobiographies are confessions; but if a man is a deep writer all his works are confessions. One of the greatest men who ever attempted an autobiography was Goethe. After his childhood, which is the readablest part of even the worst autobiography, his attempts to escape from his subject are pitiable. He takes refuge in sketches of all the Toms, Dicks, and Harrys he knew in his youth, persons utterly unmemorable, until the book drops from your hand and is not picked up again. I am one of the very few people who have read Rousseau's confessions through to the end, and can certify that from the moment when he ceases to be a rather rascally young adventurer, and becomes the great Rousseau, he might as well be anybody else for all one can grasp or remember of his everyday life.

Of Madame de Warens when he was sixteen I have a lively recollection. Of Madame d'Houdetot when he was fortyfive I have not the faintest impression, and remember only the name. In short, the confessions tell us next to nothing of any importance about the adult Rousseau. His works tell us everything we need know. If Shakespear's everyday life from his birth to his death were to come to light, and Hamlet and Mercutio to be simultaneously lost, the effect would be to substitute a perfectly commonplace man for a very interesting one. In the case of Dickens so much is known about him that might have happened to Wickens or Pickens or Stickens that his biographers have obliterated him for those who do not read his books, and for those who do, spoilt his portrait very painfully.

Therefore the autobiographical fragments which pad this volume do not present me from my own point of view, of which I am necessarily as unconscious as I am of the taste of water because it is always in my mouth. They tell you mostly what has been overlooked or misunderstood. I have pointed out, for instance, that a boy who knows the masterpieces of modern music is actually more highly educated than one who knows only the masterpieces of ancient Greek and Latin literature. I have illustrated the wretched lot in our society of the Downstart, as I call the boy-gentleman descended through younger sons from the plutocracy, for whom a university education is beyond his father's income, leaving him by family tradition a gentleman without a gentleman's means or education, and so only a penniless snob. I have thought it well to warn the young that it is as dangerous to know too much as to know too little, to be too good as to be too bad, and how Safety First lies in knowing and believing and doing what everyone knows and believes and does.

These things are mentioned not because I have been unbearably persecuted nor as yet assassinated, but because they concern my whole Downstart class, and, when intelligibly stated and understood, may help to make it class conscious and better behaved. Thus, being incorrigibly didactic, I violate the biographical laws I began this apology with by telling you little about myself that might not have happened to a thousand Shaws, and a million Smiths. Perhaps our psycho-analysts may find in such dull stuff clues that have escaped me.

To relieve the dulness there are tales of my relatives which must be read as ordinary fiction, the Irish Family Shaw having been occasionally funnier than the Swiss Family Robinson, and perhaps not less instructive to those who are capable of such instruction. As to myself, my goods are all in the bookshop window and on the stage: what is communicable has been already communicated in a long life of which, though I cannot say that no day of it has been left without a written line, yet I have perhaps brought it as near to that Roman ideal as is healthily and humanly possible.

Ayot Saint Lawrence,
  15th January 1939
    Revised 1947

3

MY MOTHER AND HER RELATIVES

MY MOTHER WAS THE
daughter of a country gentleman, and was brought up with ruthless strictness to be a paragon of all ladylike virtues and accomplishments by her grand aunt, whom I remember from my very early childhood as a humpbacked old lady with a pretty face, whose deformity seemed to me quaintly proper to her as a beneficent fairy. Had she known the magically favorable impression she made on me, she would perhaps have left me her property; and I now believe I was brought to her in the hope that I should attract her to this extent. But I was a failure. She had brought my mother up to make such a distinguished marriage as would finally wipe out an unmentionable stain on her pedigree; for though on her parents' side her extraction was everything that could be desired, her grandfather was a mysterious master spirit whose birth was so obscure that there was some doubt as to whether he ever had any legal parents at all. Under cover of the name of an employee named Cullen, he had made a fortune by

keeping a pawnshop in one of the poorest quarters of Dublin. Meanwhile, by assuming the rank of country gentleman at a "seat" in the County Dublin, he married into a genuine county family.

But still he kept the pawnshop and the pawnshop kept him; consequently my fairy great grand aunt Ellen was resolute that the daughter of her dead sister-in-law should be brought up in an unquestionably ladylike manner. So my mother had a Spartan childhood, and carried the straight-backed stamp of it to her grave. Misfortunes that would have crushed ten untrained women broke on her like waves on granite.

Nature, expelled with a fork, came back again and wrecked the life plans of her fairy aunt. When my mother grew up, she knew thoroughbass as taught by her musicmaster Johann Bernhard Logier (famous in Dublin as the inventor of the chiroplast, a mechanical finger exerciser which set his piano pupils all wrong); she could repeat two of La Fontaine's fables in French with perfect pronunciation; she could carry herself with complete dignity; and she could have worked as a ragpicker without losing her entire conviction that she was a lady, of a species apart from servants and common persons. But she could not housekeep on a small income; she had no notion of the value of money; she detested her grand aunt and regarded all that had been taught her as religion and discipline as tyranny and slavery. Consequently, as she was naturally very humane, she abandoned her own children to the most complete anarchy. Both my parents, as it happened, were utterly uncoercive.

In due time she was floated in Dublin society to get married. Among other persons with whom she came in contact was George Carr Shaw, an apparently harmless gentleman of forty, with a squint and a vein of humor which delighted in anti-climax, and would have made him an appreciative listener for Charles Lamb. He was a member of a large family which spoke of itself as "the Shaws," and got invited, on the strength of a second cousinship, to Bushy Park, the seat of the bachelor Sir Robert Shaw, Bart., as to whom see Burke's Landed Gentry. George Carr Shaw seemed very safe company for my carefully guarded mother, because nobody could conceive his having the audacity, the enterprise, nor the means, to marry anybody, even if it could be supposed that his years or his squint could appeal to so well brought-up a female as Miss Lucinda Elizabeth Gurly. He was therefore well spoken of to her by her relatives as a quite eligible person to know in a general social way. They forgot that, having never been taught what marriage really means, nor experienced impecuniosity, she might marry any adventurer without knowing how much she was doing.

Her tragedy came about by external pressure of a sort that nobody could have foreseen.

Her widowed father most unexpectedly married again: this time the penniless daughter of an old friend of his whose bills he had backed with ruinous consequences. The alliance

25

did not please the family of his first wife, especially his brother-in-law, a Kilkenny squire, to whom he owed money, and from whom he concealed his intention to marry again.

Unfortunately my mother innocently let out the secret to her uncle. The consequence was that my grandfather, going out on his wedding morning to buy a pair of gloves for the ceremony, was arrested for debt at the suit of his brother-in-law. One can hardly blame him for being furious. But his fury carried him beyond all reason. He believed that my mother had betrayed him deliberately so as to stop the marriage by his arrest. My mother, who was on a visit to some relatives in Dublin at the time, had to choose between two homes to return to. One was the house of a stepmother and an enraged father. The other was the house of her aunt, which meant the old domestic slavery and tyranny.

It was at this moment that some devil, perhaps commissioned by the Life Force to bring me into the world, prompted my father to propose marriage to Miss Bessie Gurly. She caught at the straw. She had heard that he had a pension of £60 a year; and to her, who had never been allowed to have more than pocket money nor to housekeep, £60 seemed an enormous and inexhaustible sum. She calmly announced her engagement, dropping the bombshell as unconcernedly as if it were a colored glass ball from her solitaire board. People played solitaire in those days.

Finding it impossible to make her see the gravity of the pecuniary situation, or to induce her to cancel her engagement on such a ground, her people played another card. They told her that George Carr Shaw was a drunkard. She indignantly refused to believe them, reminding them that they had never objected to him before. When they persisted, she went to him straightforwardly and asked him was it true. He assured her most solemnly that he was a convinced and lifelong teetotaller. And she believed him and married him. But it was true. He drank.

Without attempting to defend my father for telling this whopper, I must explain that he really was in principle a convinced teetotaller. Unfortunately it was the horror of his own experience as an occasional dipsomaniac that gave him this conviction, which he was miserably unable to carry into practice.

I can only imagine the hell into which my mother descended when she found out what shabby-genteel poverty with a drunken husband is like. She told me once that when they were honeymooning in Liverpool (of all places) she opened her bridegroom's wardrobe and found it full of empty bottles. In the first shock of the discovery she ran away to the docks to get employed as a stewardess and be taken out of the country. But on the way she was molested by some rough docklanders and had to run back again.

I have elsewhere recorded how, when my father, taking me for a walk, pretended in play to throw me into the canal, he very nearly did it. When we got home I said to my mother as an awful and hardly credible discovery "Mamma: I think

Papa is drunk." This was too much for her. She replied
"When is he anything else?"

It is a rhetorical exaggeration to say that I have never since
believed in anything or anybody; but the wrench from my
childish faith in my father as perfect and omniscient to the
discovery that he was a hypocrite and a dipsomaniac was so
sudden and violent that it must have left its mark on me.

Her aunt cut her off ruthlessly in spite of my infant charms.
All my mother had from her was an earlier gift of a bundle
of I.O.U.s signed by my grandfather. She was innocent
enough to let him see them and ask what she should do with
them. He promptly put them into the fire. This did not
matter, as he would not have paid them anyhow; but he also
tried to use a power of appointment under her grandfather's
(the pawnbroker's) will to deprive her of any share of his
bequests to his grandchildren; and though the Gurly family
solicitor rescued some £40 a year for her by absolutely
refusing to allow him to do his worst, it left my mother
convinced that her father was a vindictive parent, not too
scrupulously conscientious in money matters.

Then there was her brother, my maternal Uncle Walter.
But he was dissolute, and had offended her once by being
savagely violent to her in a fit of temper. He went their
father's feckless way as to the property. Everybody had disappointed her, or betrayed her, or tyrannized over her.

She was not at all soured by all this. She never made scenes,
never complained, never nagged, never punished nor retali-

ated nor lost her self-control nor her superiority to spites and tantrums and tempers. She was neither weak nor submissive; but as she never revenged, so also she never forgave. There were no quarrels and consequently no reconciliations. You did a wrong; and you were classed by her as a person who did such wrongs, and tolerated indulgently up to a point. But if at last you drove her to break with you, the breach was permanent: you did not get back again. Among my *Maxims for Revolutionists* there is "Beware of the man who does not return your blow." From my mother I had learned that the wrath on which the sun goes down is negligible compared to the clear vision and criticism that is neither created by anger nor ended with it.

Under all the circumstances it says a great deal for my mother's humanity that she did not hate her children. She did not hate anybody, nor love anybody. The specific maternal passion awoke in her a little for my younger sister, who died at 20; but it did not move her until she lost her, nor then noticeably. She did not concern herself much about us; for she had never been taught that mothering is a science, nor that it matters in the least what children eat or drink: she left all that to servants whose wage was £8 a year and could neither write nor read. She had no sense of the value of her own training, and gave it no credit for its results, which she may have regarded as gifts of nature; but she had a deep sense of its cruelties. As we grew up and had to take care of ourselves unguided, we met life's difficulties by breaking our shins over them, gaining such wisdom as was inevitable by making fools of ourselves. On the whole it was easier for my mother than her aunt's plan; and it was certainly meant to be kinder: in fact it was very much kinder, but not so much so as she thought. Letting a calf stray into every china shop is not the only alternative to goading it along the street. In short, my mother was, from the technical point of view of a modern welfare worker, neither a mother nor a wife, and could be classed only as a Bohemian anarchist with ladylike habits.

My father was impecunious and unsuccessful: he could do nothing that interested her; and he did not shake off his miserable and disgraceful tippling (he did eventually) until it was too late to make any difference in their relations. Had there not been imagination, idealization, the charm of music, the charm of lovely seas and sunsets, and our natural kindliness and gentleness, it is impossible to say what cynical barbarism we might not have grown into.

My mother's salvation came through music. She had a mezzosoprano voice of extraordinary purity of tone; and to cultivate it she took lessons from George John Vandaleur Lee, already well established in Dublin as an orchestral conductor, an organizer of concerts, and a teacher of singing so heterodox and original that he depended for his performances on amateurs trained by himself, and was detested by his professional rivals, whom he disparaged as voice wreckers, as indeed they mostly were. He extended this criticism to doctors, and amazed us by eating brown bread instead of white, and sleeping with the window open, both of which habits I acquired and have practised ever since. His influence in our household, of which he at last became a member, accustomed me to the scepticism as to academic authority which still persists in me.

He not only made my mother sing by a method that preserved her voice perfectly until her death at over eighty but gave her a Cause and a Creed to live for.

Those who know my play Misalliance, in which the lover has three fathers, will note that I also had a natural father and two supplementaries, making three varieties for me to study. This widened my outlook very considerably. Natural parents should bear in mind that the more supplementaries their children find, at school or elsewhere, the better they will know that it takes all sorts to make a world. Also that though there is always the risk of being corrupted by bad parents, the natural ones may be—probably ten per cent. of them actually are—the worst of the lot.

Then there was my maternal Uncle Walter. During my boyhood he was a ship's surgeon on the Inman line (now the American), visiting us between voyages. He had been educated at Kilkenny College, in his time the Eton of Ireland. When he was the smallest boy there, and the only one who could squeeze himself out under the locked college gates, he was sent by the elder boys at night into the town to make assignations for them with ladies of the street, his reward being whisky enough to make him insensibly drunk. (He was, by the way, astonished and horrified by the homosexualities of English public schools, and maintained that schools should always be, like Kilkenny College, within reach of women.) From Trinity College in Dublin, his university, he had had to retire to recuperate after excessive dissipation. Then, as his father, always short of money through backing bills for his friends and recklessly mortgaging, could not support him, he qualified as a surgeon and took the Inman job. He could learn subjects for examination and pass them easily enough, and was apparently an efficient medical officer under discipline.

He was a most exhilarating person, because he had, like my mother, though without her dignity, a youthfulness that no dissipation could exhaust, and was robust and fullblooded. His profanity and obscenity in conversation were of Rabelaisian exuberance; and as to the *maxima reverentia* due to my tender years, he had rather less of it, if possible, than Falstaff had for Prince Hal. To the half dozen childish rhymes taught me by my mother he added a stock of unprintable limericks that constituted almost an education in geography. He was always in high spirits, and full of a humor that, though barbarous in its blasphemous indecency, was Scriptural and Shakespearean in the elaboration and fantasy of its literary expression. Being full of the Bible, he quoted the sayings of Jesus as models of facetious repartee. He considered Anthony Trollope's novels the only ones worth reading (in those days they were regarded as daring exposures

"SHAW'S ASTONISHING AND ADMIRABLE MOTHER"

Lord Olivier in his autobiography

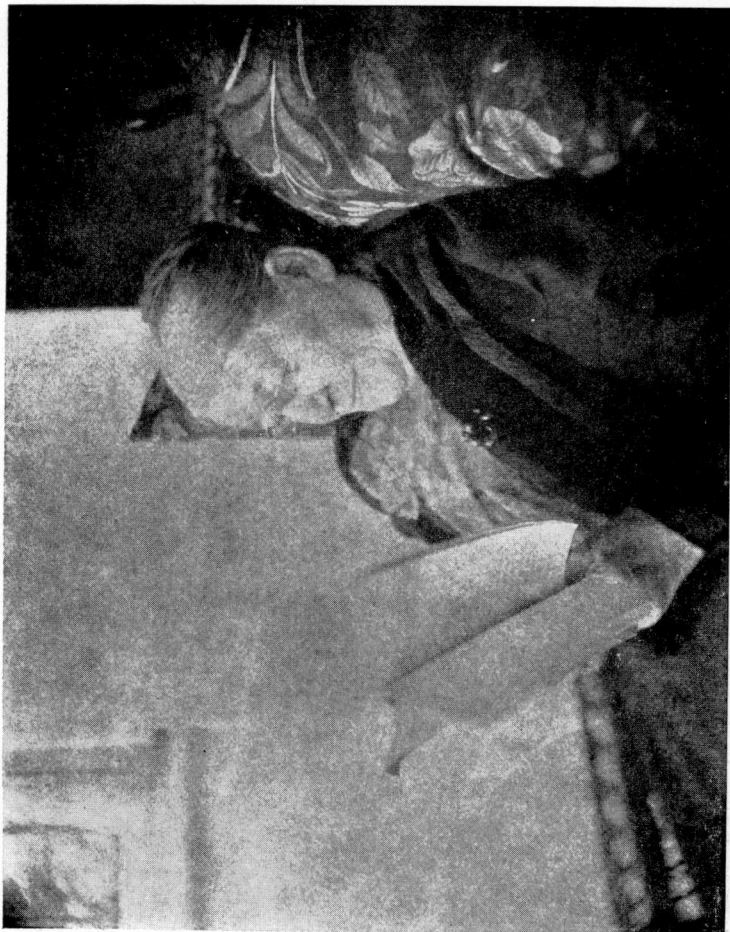

MY LAST PORTRAITS

OF MY MOTHER

GEORGE JOHN VANDALEUR LEE

Eminent Dublin orchestral conductor who taught my mother the method of singing she taught me. Photographed by Richard Pigott, repeatedly imprisoned for sedition as editor of The Irishman, and finally infamous as forger of the Parnell letters of the Church!); and his favorite opera was Auber's Fra Diavolo. Possibly if he had been cultivated artistically in his childhood, he would have been a man of refined pleasures, and might have done something in literature. As it was, he was a scoffer and a rake, because no better pleasures had ever been either revealed or denied to him. In spite of his excesses, which were not continuous, being the intermittent debauches of a seafarer on shore, he was an upstanding healthy man until he married an English widow in America and settled as a general practitioner in Leyton, Essex, then a country district on the borders of Epping Forest. His wife tried to make him behave himself according to English lights: to go to church; to consult the feelings and prejudices of his patients; to refrain from the amusement of scandalizing their respectability; or at least to stint himself in the item of uproarious blasphemy. It was quite useless: her protests only added to the zest of his profanities. Nevertheless, he held his own in Leyton county society because he was very amusing, and was perceptibly a gentleman who drove his own horse and had bought his select practice.

Soon, however, east London spread and swallowed up Leyton. The country houses of his patients were demolished and replaced by rows of little brick boxes inhabited by clerks in tall hats supporting families on fifteen shillings a week. The change ruined my uncle. His wife died in disgust and despair, leaving everything she possessed to the relatives of her former husband. His horse was sold; his watch was

33

pawned; his clothes became disgracefully shabby; and when he died, and I inherited his estate, I found that the wages of the one servant who had stuck to him through it all had not been paid for seventeen years. His father had long before mortgaged the estate up to the hilt; and I should have had to repudiate my inheritance of it had it come to me a few years earlier. As it was, I was able to pay off the mortgages, rebuild the wrecked houses, support the poor relations, and restore the estate to solvency. Finally I municipalized it, having to procure an Act of the Dail (the parliament of Eire) to enable me to do so, or anyone else to follow my example.

The children of Bohemian Anarchists are often in such strenuous reaction against their bringing-up that they are the most tyrannically conventional of parents. The problem of how much and when children can be kindly and safely left to their own devices, and how much guided and ordered, is the most difficult part of parental policy. Prince Peter Kropotkin, a comprehensive thinker, far above the average in wisdom and kindliness, said of children "You can only look on." My mother, if she had ever thought about the matter at all, would have said "You can only go your own way and let the children go theirs." But there can be no such rule of thumb. The line between tutelage and freethought varies from individual to individual. Even within the same family one child can do next to nothing until it is told what to do until it adolesces, when it does what everybody else does. Its brother or sister may be so unbiddable that it must either be left to the police as a criminal or allowed its own way as a freethinking genius.

The degrees between these extremes are micrometrical. No child can be governed so completely as to have no will of its own: the task would be too much for any parent. But a child left to do anything it likes at all ages and on all occasions will swallow matches or set the house on fire with them, and refuse to learn the alphabet and the multiplication table. On the whole it is safer to delegate the child's education to a conventional school, as Voltaire's was to the Jesuits, leaving it to react by its own strength, than to risk its having to learn with difficulty in its sixteenth year what it could have been taught easily in its sixth.

Chances must be taken in any case. A child cannot be trained in Europe for a higher rank than that of the Papal Chair. But its trainer may be asked "What sort of Pope? Gregory the Great or Alexander Borgia? Pius IX or Leo XIII?" The aim may be rather to produce a great citizen and civilizer. If so, it will still be a toss-up whether the result will be a Sidney Webb or a Bakunin.

Neither my parents nor my schoolmasters ever asked themselves such questions; and had I not had the rare luck to make money as a born playwright I might now be ending as a tramp. Much that I should have been taught in my nonage I had to teach myself later; and much that I was taught I had to unlearn. So I can only repeat that the frontier between tutelage and freethought is hard to find, and is not, as a law

35

must be, the same for everybody.

Yet there must be law in large families and in all schools. This complicates the problem beyond any cut and dried solution that I can suggest. Schools at present make a worse mess of it than households. As I write I have before me a letter from a clever little girl in an Irish convent school. She proudly gives me a list of her nine simultaneous school classes in different languages and branches of education, the acquirement of each of which would be a whole time job for many months for a budding Newton. Such a curriculum leaves me speechless. Yet it must not be inferred that I am on the side of those who agitate against what they call premature educational pressure. John Stuart Mill was taught the classical dead languages when he was a child by his father James Mill. I have heard James denounced as a monster for this by William Morris. But I am not so sure. John himself was not so sure. I am not defending the current assumption in the plutocratic public schools that a man is educated when he can read Latin and solve quadratic equations. Obviously he may be able to do both and remain dangerously ignorant as a citizen. And mostly, when he has been crammed and coached into a university degree on this assumption, he may never again look at a page of Latin or think of it without loathing, nor keep his accounts in any but the simplest arithmetic. Yet I am faced with the flat fact that most of us (including myself) remember only the paradigms we have been taught in our childhood, however deeply we may philosophize in later life.

My memory of the multiplication and pence tables I learnt before I was six, and the Latin declensions and conjugations I learnt before I was ten, I still remember in my ninetysecond year, whereas my efforts as an adult to memorize similar paradigms in modern languages were so unsuccessful that I advise students of them not to waste time in trying to learn irregular verbs (the Spanish ones, for instance) but to speak them as regular. Spaniards may laugh; but they will understand, which is all that is necessary. When an English child says "I thinked" and "I goed" it is just as well understood as if it said "I thought" and "I went." Pidgin is as useful as the English of Milton, and much more concise. Our craze for standards of correctness, pushed as it is to make any departure from them a punishable moral delinquency, wastes years of our lives. However many ways are open before us we refuse to move until two of them are labelled respectively right and wrong, with the right as difficult as we can make it and the wrong the shortest and easiest.

4

SHAME AND WOUNDED SNOBBERY

A SECRET KEPT FOR 80 YEARS

I NOW CONFESS TO AN episode in my boyhood formerly so repugnant to me that for 80 years I never mentioned it to any mortal creature, not even to my wife. It was to me what the blacking warehouse was to Dickens. His intense shame of that brief episode is too easily discounted as class snobbery; and so for a time I discounted my own abhorred secret. But in fact it was most instructive, and explains my utter rejection of the accepted plan for providing secondary education by sending proletarian winners of scholarships to proprietarian public schools (so called), and absorbing them into the service of the capitalist class after imbuing them thoroughly with the capitalist outlook on society. The proletarian thus promoted is often the most reactionary of Old School Ties. My verdict is that proletarian children should be sent to really public proletarian secondary schools, and that their contacts with young

Etonians, Harrovians, Wykeham boys, and Rugbeians should be limited to street fights with them. The old school tie of a proletarian school should be as proudly flaunted and jealously cherished as any capitalist tie, and confer as high a degree of culture, or higher. I base this conclusion on the experience I now for the first time avow.

My first lessons in Latin in the interval between being taught to read and write by a governess (and taught very well) and my going to school, took place privately in the house of my clerical uncle-in-law William George Carroll, where I sat with his two sons and learnt the declensions and conjugations and irregular verbs quite easily; so that when I went to school at what is now Wesley College, and was then the Wesleyan Connexional School, I at once rose to the head of the First Latin Junior.

At School I learnt nothing from the curriculum, and at last forgot a good deal of what my uncle had taught me, although the school, snobbishly preparatory for the university, took no subjects seriously except Latin and Greek, with a pretence of mathematics (Euclidean), of English history (mostly false and scurrilous), and some nominal geography of which I have no recollection. The classes were too large, and the teachers, untrained in pedagogy, mostly picking up a living on their way to becoming Wesleyan ministers. Not a word was said to us about the meaning or utility of mathematics: we were simply asked to explain how an equilateral triangle could be constructed by the intersection of two circles, and to do sums in *a*, *b*, and *x* instead of in pence and shillings, leaving me so ignorant that I concluded that *a* and *b* must mean eggs and cheese and *x* nothing, with the result that I rejected algebra as nonsense, and never changed that opinion until in my advanced twenties Graham Wallas and Carl Pearson convinced me that instead of being taught mathematics I had been made a fool of.

Euclid gave me no trouble: the asses' bridge did not bother me; so though I was a confirmed idler I was expected to do well in the examinations. Unfortunately the examination questions stated, not the problems, but their numbers in the book, of which I knew nothing, having picked up all the solutions in class; so I failed disgracefully.

Only in literature did the school establish a claim to have foreseen my future celebrity. We were set to write essays; and I got a first class for a very florid description of the Liffey pool below bridges; but no prize nor serious importance was attached to this or to any subject but Latin.

There was only one method of teaching. Instead of the pupil asking, and the teacher answering and explaining, the teacher asked the questions. If the pupil could not give the book answer, he received a bad mark, and at the end of the week expiated it by suffering not more than six "tips" (slaps across the palm with a cane) which did not hurt sufficiently to do more than convince me that corporal punishment, to be effective, must be cruel.

After some years of this imprisonment, which though educationally null, at least took me for half the day off the hands of my parents at home, my clerical uncle examined me, and found that I was learning nothing, and forgetting what he had taught me. I was taken away from the Wesleyan, and sent to a very private school in Glasthule, between Kingstown and Dalkey, kept by a family named Halpin. There was an end of this when we presently moved back from our villeggiatura in Dalkey (pronounced Dawky) to Dublin.

Then came my snob tragedy. I have elsewhere described how our household was shared by George John Vandaleur Lee, mesmeric conductor and daringly original teacher of singing, who was my mother's musical tutor and colleague. My parents seem hardly to have considered whether I was educated or not, provided I went to school according to custom. But Lee, though almost wholly preoccupied with music, thought that something ought to be done about it; for I was clearly learning nothing except what I had better not have learnt. It happened that just then he made the acquaintance of a certain Mr. Peach, who was drawing master at the Central Model Boys' School in Marlborough Street, undenominational and classless in theory but in fact Roman Catholic, where the boys whose parents could afford it brought five shillings to school periodically, and were caned in the Wesleyan manner if they failed. It was an enormous place, with huge unscaleable railings and gates on which for me might well have been inscribed "All hope abandon, ye who enter here"; for that the son of a Protestant merchant-gentleman and feudal downstart should pass those bars or associate in any way with its hosts of lower middle class Catholic children, sons of petty shopkeepers and tradesmen, was inconceivable from the Shaw point of view.

But Peach had impressed on Lee that the teaching, as far as it went, was skilled and genuine, and that the cheaper genteel private schools were worse than useless. So I was sent to Marlborough Street, and at once lost caste outside it and became a boy with whom no Protestant young gentleman would speak or play.

Not so within the railings. There I was a superior being, and in play hour did not play, but walked up and down with the teachers in their reserved promenade.

It did not last long. I was in my thirteenth year (1869) and endured it from February to September. I for the first time set myself against my fate, and flatly refused to go back to the Model School on any terms. My father, as much ashamed of it as I was, and much less resolute, let me have my way; and I was duly restored to genteel Protestantism in a day school of the Incorporated Society For Promoting Protestant School in Ireland. It was in Aungier Street (pronounced Ainjer) and labelled Dublin English Scientific and Commercial Day School. It was closed in 1878. This was my last school prison. I left it in 1871 to become, in my fifteenth year, junior clerk in a highly exclusive gentlemanly estate office crowded with premium paying apprentices who, being mostly university graduates, were fully up to Shaw standards of gentility, and were addressed as Mister whilst I was plain Shaw.

My school bill in Aungier Street was £4 a quarter, plus four shillings for drawing, which was an extra, and was the only extra my parents ever thought of paying for. The drawing master made no pretence of teaching or keeping order. Once a week a clergyman held a bible class, at which we played all sorts of tricks on him and never dreamt of taking religion seriously.

I am not sure that if Marlborough Street had been explained to me as an experimental model school for pupils, not of the laboring "common people" but for the children of persons of modest means engaged in retail instead of wholesale trade, Catholic or Protestant, I might have been spared all my shame; for I was already in revolt against the Shaw snobbery, and observant of the fact that my father's tailor had a country house in Dalkey, a yacht in Dalkey Sound, and could afford to send his sons, much better dressed and equipped than I, to expensive preparatory schools and to college. To rank him as socially inferior to my impecunious father, whose bills were never paid punctually, was as patently absurd to me at 12½ years of age as it is now in my nineties. Far from being a Protestant bigot I was a Boy Atheist, and proud of it, having quite deliberately given up praying as an irrational practice. And my mother's musical activities had cured me of social prejudice against Roman Catholics as well as of my inculcated belief that they all went to hell when they died. My political leanings were flatly Fenian. I was not unreasonable: quite the contrary. I was far too open to reason.

All the same, the facts were too stubborn. The classes would not mix. Only sufficient equality of income to make classes intermarriageable will break down class segregation; and in my boyhood it had not yet done so. It has done so since only where the incomes are big. Many years after I shook the dust of the Model School from my feet I lunched one day, an honored guest, at the house of Viscount Powerscourt, an aristocrat among Irish aristocrats. When his daughter left the party early to go up to Dublin it was apologetically explained to me that she had to do so because she was going that evening to a ball at the house of Sir John Arnot, a mammoth Dublin shopkeeper.

I was amazed. In my time she could not have spoken to a shopkeeper, except across the counter, without being ostracized as completely as I was when I was planted out at the Model School, not knowing that it was a model school, and taking it for a common "National School" for the poorest and lowest. But this was never explained to me. Nothing was explained to me. I have been finding out for myself ever since.

Why did the Model School afflict me with a shame which was more or less a psychosis. I have told elsewhere that my esthetic hatred of poverty and squalor, and of the species of human animal they produce, was acquired not at the Model

45

School, where the boys were not worse clad and fed than I, but in the slums into which my nursemaid took me on her visits to her friends when she was supposed to be exercising me in the parks. I hated these experiences intensely. My artist nature, to which beauty and refinement were necessities, would not accept poor people as fellowcreatures, nor slum tenements as fit for human habitation. To me they were places where I could not possibly live. The mental process thus set up culminated some fifty years later in my play Major Barbara, in which the millionaire saint, Andrew Undershaft, thunders his doctrine that poverty is not the natural and proper punishment of vice, but a social crime compared to which our sporadic murders and thefts are negligible. Later still, when my famous bacteriologist friend Sir Almroth Wright remarked disparagingly that he believed that the effect of sanitation in abolishing disease is purely esthetic, I agreed heartily, and maintained that he had hit on a discovery that would eclipse all his famous contributions to the natural history of microbes.

Finally, a point to be scored by our psycho-analysts. Although for eighty years I never could bring myself to mention the Marlborough Street episode, yet now that I have broken through the habit of ashamed silence, and made not only a clean breast of it but a clear brain, I am completely cured. There is not a vestige of my boyish shame left: it survives not as a complex but a habit flicked off without the slightest difficulty.

46

This illustrates the failures and successes of psychotherapy. Inculcated habits being traumatic, are curable: inborn complexes, no. If a child is told any story, however absurd or impossible, by someone whom it regards as infallible (mostly a parent), it will accept it as gospel truth and hold it thoughtlessly until it is driven to reason about it, which may possibly never happen. When I was told in childhood that a Mr Haughton who paid us a visit was a Unitarian, I asked my father what a Unitarian was. He replied humorously that the Unitarians believed that Jesus was not crucified, but was seen running away down the other side of the Hill of Calvary. I believed this for nearly thirty years.

My own childish mistakes stuck to me like my father's jokes. My mistaking the *a, b, n,* and *x* of the school algebra for goods instead of quantities was one of them. People's minds are full of these survivals from their childhood. When (if ever) they discard them they are apt to imagine that the facts on which they base their change of mind are new to them. Mostly these facts have been staring them in the face all their lives. When I first in my boyhood gave up my inculcated belief that the Bible was the literally inspired and dictated word of an omniscient and infallible anthropomorphic god, I compromized by secularizing the Old Testament but not the New. It was I who was changing: not the evidence. At present the glaring fact that Jehovah is a tribal idol barbarously different from Jesus's "Our Father which art in heaven" has not yet cured Christians of calling Jehovah and

Jesus God Almighty indiscriminately.

Now that so many Cabinet Ministers and Secretaries of State come from ungentlemanly proletarian schools it may not be easy for English, Scottish and American readers to understand why I should have made a guilty secret of the Model School. But where there is poverty there is still no change. Manual laborers and gentlemen remain distinct species. It was far worse in Ireland when I was born. Railway carriages were first, second, and third class; and ladies and gentlemen could not travel third class. There were no cushions in the third class. Male passengers smoked shag, and expectorated in all directions. They wore corduroys tied at the knee, collarless shirts which had been left so long unwashed that they offended the second class nose. None of them could read or write: to them the Model School was an aristocratic middle class university beyond their utmost social aspirations. In town they lived in slum tenements: in the country they shared mud-floored cabins with their livestock, or rented dilapidated cowhouses. Their schools, when they had any, were called Ragged Schools; and their women wore shoes and socks only on great occasions when they attended a fair or a religious service. Nevertheless they were human, sometimes to a saintly degree, and just as much divided into categories of Nature's gentry and Nature's cads as the House of Lords. They were full of their own class snobberies, as those of us know who have tried to establish Women's Institutes in English villages and found that none of the women

MY BLASPHEMOUS RABELAISIAN UNCLE

Dr. Walter John Gurly

RAILINGS OF THE CENTRAL MODEL SCHOOL. MY PRISON BARS

would meet oneanother as social equals.

But, I must repeat, such common humanities did not make the classes associable. In any house large enough to have a kitchen and a drawing-room the pet dog was as much at home with the servants as with their employers; but the human animals were immovably segregate. I was born in a house where there was a kitchen and a drawing-room, and always at least one "thorough-servant," paid £8 a year in cash, and lodged in the basement.

Thus the extremes of class segregation, however modified by advancing Socialism, are still rampant. In countries where the vast majority of proletarians are black or brown or yellow, there is no pretence of equality nor even of human similarity. And I maintain that the remedy is not to force all the sections into the old institutions, but to face the fact of their segregation and tolerate proletarian schools, lower middle class schools, Etonian caste schools, Jim Crow cars and the like, with the difference that whereas social promotion is now regarded as a matter of enabling County Council and Polytechnic scholarship winners to break into the Etonian preserves, they should "keep themselves to themselves" and assert, not their equality but their superiority as chosen races on all possible or pretended grounds. The negro, far from objecting to the Jim Crow car, should insist on it, and on the exclusion from it of "poor whites." The Jew should confront the anti-Semites, not as equals, but as Joshua confronted the Canaanites, as a superior being divinely chosen to govern them. Only on these

49

lines will they cultivate themselves to the point at which their pretensions become so patently ridiculous and their culture so general and identical that intermarriageable equality will establish itself, as it had already done when I found Irish Viscounts on visiting terms with Irish Selfridges.

The Incorporated Society's School, though cheap and Protestant and genteel like the Wesleyan, did not pretend to be preparatory for university graduation, and frankly excluded classics from its curriculum. It was for pupils whose fathers, like my own, could not afford to send them to Trinity College, and aimed no higher than to have them trained not for scholarship but for business. Two or three older boys who had a special aptitude for higher mathematics sat apart, not in class, and taught themselves; for nobody else even pretended to teach them. The headmaster sat in his study and had no contact with the boys except when they were sent there to be caned. He was hastily preparing himself for ordination in the then Established Protestant Episcopal Church of Ireland so that he might be qualified for "commutation" when Gladstone disestablished it. The teaching method was the Wesleyan all over again.

I, however, was not the same person I had been at the Wesleyan. The natural growth which I have described in my play Man and Superman as the birth of moral passion had taken place in me. At the Wesleyan I had never dreamt of learning my lessons, nor of telling the truth to that common enemy and executioner, the schoolmaster. My scruples began in the Model School; and in Aungier Street, lying was beneath my new moral dignity as a head boy, a position which I shared with a schoolfellow named Dunne who had been with me at the Wesleyan, and had developed a precocity so extraordinary that at sixteen or thereabouts he had the bearing and moral weight of a bishop. So I had to keep up my credit by doing my class work (very trifling) consci-entiously. I had only one conflict with the school discipline. Some offence was committed; and the master, to discover whom to punish, asked each boy in succession whether he was the culprit. I refused to answer on the ground that no boy was legally bound to criminate himself, and that the interrogation was a temptation to boys to lie. A day or two passed during which I was supposed to be doomed to some appalling punishment; but I heard no more of it: the situation was new to the teaching staff. When authorities do not know what to do, they can only do what was done last time. As I had created an unprecedented situation, they did nothing; but there were no more such interrogatories. It was my first re-form.

At the Model School I had already asserted myself in another direction. The reading lessons in history ignored Ireland and glorified England. I always substituted Ireland for England in such dithyrambs. The boys wondered what would happen to me. But the teacher smiled and said nothing. I was, in fact, a young Fenian in my political sympathies, such as they were.

51

One more Aungier Street incident. Through the sudden illness of the Head's wife, my classroom was left for more than an hour without the surveillance of a master, who ordered us not to make a noise. We kept quiet for perhaps a minute. Then we "went Fantee," roaring, and wrecking everything wreckable in the room. I did as the rest did.

The experience was not lost on me. Many years later I was to see the same thing happen twice among adults, once to a company of first class passengers on a liner, and once at a Fabian Society spree. It did not surprise me to see it depicted in a Russian educational film. It taught me how thin is the veneer of bourgeois civilization, and why I, no more than Shakespear or Dickens, can be persuaded that, without natural leaders and rulers, democratic civilization can be achieved under the pretext of Liberty by Unlimited Suffrage for unqualified nobodies elected by politically uneducated everybodies, even when the first elected nobodies are Napoleons. As likely as not they would be only Hitlers.

5

MY OFFICE-BOYHOOD

IN A GILBERT AND SUL-
livan opera a promoted British office boy tells us how he
cleaned the windows and swept the floor and polished up the
handle of the big front door. I did nothing so ungentlemanly.
The office was that of a highly genteel firm of Irish estate
agents (in Ireland then estate agency ranked as a profession).
Having the introduction of my uncle Frederick, chief of the
Land Valuation Office, without whose goodwill estate agents
would have been gravely hampered, I could not engage in
manual labor of any kind, and called myself junior clerk.
For £18 a year I filed the incoming letters and found them
when required. Of the outgoing letters I took impressions in
a copying press before posting them. The only account I kept
was the postage account. I was Errand Boy to the extent of
taking leases to the Custom House to be stamped, and so
experienced the Circumlocution Office incivility I had read
about in Little Dorrit. My lunch was a penny roll; and as I
had to go out to buy this, I bought for the rest of the staff

as well. At that time luncheon was not a serious meal: at most it was only a snack. Later in life I came up against old actors who knew nothing of it and could not understand why rehearsals should be interrupted for it or young players knock off work for it.

No more than at school was anything explained to me. If some odd job puzzled me I was told to "see what was done last time"; and to this I owe my knowledge of how necessary political Constitutions are in the long intervals between able monarchs, leaders, or dictators, when the authorities can think of nothing except continuing an established routine. I had the rare faculty for learning and generalizing from experience, though I did not then know that it was rare, and attached no importance to it. I took not the slightest interest in land agency; but I laid up a large stock of observations which became useful when Henry George explained their political significance to me. At the time I simply disliked business, and did not think politically about it.

At the end of about a year, a sudden vacancy occurred in the most active post in the office: that of head cashier. As this involved banking business for the clients, and the daily receipt and payment of cheques and all sorts of rents, interests, insurances, and private allowances, it was a bustling post, and a position of trust as well. The vacancy occurred so suddenly that I had to stop the gap pending the engagement of a new cashier of mature age and high character. But as I found no difficulty in doing the work, and succeeded in changing my sloped, straggly, boyish handwriting for a very fair imitation of the compact script of my predecessor; and as, furthermore, the doubling of my salary (now £24) to £48 was a considerable step ahead, the engagement of a mature cashier was first delayed, and then dropped. I proved a conscientiously correct cashier and accountant. Though I never knew how much money I had in the pocket I reserved for my own private cash, I was never a farthing out in my office accounts. And so I was no longer an office boy. I was chief cashier, head cashier, sole cashier, equal to any of the staff, and the most active and responsible member of it.

But my heart was not in the business. I never made a payment without a hope that I should never have to make it again. Yet I was so wanting in enterprise, and shy and helpless in worldly matters (though I believe I had the air of being rather the reverse) that every six months I found myself making the payment again.

On the other hand, the office secured for me the society of a set of gentlemen apprentices, who had paid big premiums to be taught a genteel profession. They learnt little for their money except the scraps of operas I taught them. I recall one occasion when an apprentice, perched on the washstand with his face shewing above the screen that decently concealed it and stood for Manrico's tower dungeon, sang *Ah, che la morte* so passionately that he was unconscious of the sudden entry of the senior partner, Charles Uniacke Townshend, who stared stupended at the bleating countenance above the screen, and finally fled upstairs, completely beaten by the situation.

Thus I had in the office some fun and the society of university men; but I hated my position and my work; and in 1876, I walked out and threw myself recklessly into London, joining my mother there immediately after the death of my sister Agnes in the Isle of Wight.

One or two other things I may as well mention. A little time after I entered the office the appalling discovery was made that instead of being a Protestant church-goer, as became a youth introduced by a high official in the Valuation Office, I was actually what used to be called in those days an Infidel. Arguments arose in which I, being young and untrained in dialectic, got severely battered. "What is the use," said Humphrey Lloyd (an apprentice), "of arguing when you dont know what a syllogism is?" I went to the dictionary and found out what it was, learning, like Molière's bourgeois hero, that I had been syllogizing all my life without knowing it. On the matter coming to the ears of my senior employer Charles Uniacke Townshend, a pillar of the Church, of the Royal Dublin Society, and of everything else pillarable in Dublin, he respected my freedom of conscience so far as to make no attempt to reason with me nor interfere with my religion or irreligion; but he demanded a promise not to discuss the subject in his office. Against my conscience I gave him my word, and kept it, not because my living was at stake (I have never hesitated to burn my boats) but because

I did not intend to live under such limitations permanently. The incident put land-agency and office life out of the question for me as a serious career. I remained ashamed of my promise; and when my employers after I left gave me a handsome testimonial at my father's request I was unreasonably furious that such a demand should have been made. I am now (1947) rather proud of the document.

Nevertheless I was by no means clearly conscious of my own value and destiny. But one day the apprentice who sang *Ah, che la morte* so passionately happened to remark that every boy thinks he is going to be a great man. The shock that this gave me made me suddenly aware that this was my own predicament, though I could do nothing that gave me the smallest ground for classing myself as born to the hierarchy of Shakespear, Shelley, Mozart, Praxiteles, and Michael Angelo. Such a pretence in a promoted office boy seemed monstrous: my youthful diffidence and cowardice told me I was only an ignorant duffer. But my desk and cashbox gave me the habit of daily work, and taught me that I must learn to do something instead of daydreaming, and that nothing but technical skill, practice, efficiency: in short, mastery, could be of any use to me. The sort of *aplomb* my cousins seemed to derive from the consciousness that their great-great-grandfathers had also been the great-great-grandfathers of Sir Robert Shaw of Bushy Park was denied to me. You cannot be imposed on by baronets as such if you belong to the republic of art. I was chronically ashamed and unhappy because I could not do anything I wanted to do. I could keep Uniacke Townshend's cash and never dream of stealing it (riper years have made me aware that many of my artistic feats may be less highly estimated in the books of the Recording Angel); but at the time it counted for less than nothing. It was a qualification for what I hated.

My literary activity during this time, though I did not count it as such, had begun. An old schoolfellow of mine, Matthew Edward McNulty, later the author of three novels of Irish life, was an official in the Bank of Ireland, and had been drafted to the Newry branch of that institution. We had struck up a friendship, being both imaginative geniuses, although circumstances separated us so effectually that after our schooldays we saw no more of one another. But during these boyish years we kept up a correspondence by return of post, writing immense letters to one another illustrated with crude drawings and enlivened by burlesque dramas. It was understood that the letters were to be destroyed as soon as answered, as we did not like the possibility of our unreserved soul histories falling into strange hands.

I also made a most valuable acquaintance through the accident of coming to lodge in the same house with him. This was Chichester Bell, a cousin of Graham Bell, the inventor of the telephone, consequently a nephew of Melville Bell the inventor of the phonetic script known as Visible speech. His father was Alexander Bell, author of the Standard Elocutionist, and by far the most majestic and imposing man that ever

58

lived on this or any other planet. He had been elocution professor in my old school, the Wesleyan Connexional, now Wesley College. Chichester Bell was a qualified physician who had gone to Germany and devoted himself to chemistry and physics in the school of Helmholtz. My intercourse with him was of great use to me. We studied Italian together; and though I did not learn Italian I learned a good deal else, mostly about physics and pathology. I read Tyndall and Trousseau's Clinical Lectures. And it was Bell who made me take Wagner seriously. I had heard nothing of his except the Tannhäuser march played by a second-rate military band; and my only comment was that the second theme was a weak imitation of the famous air, made up of a chain of turns, in Weber's Freischütz overture. When I found that Bell regarded Wagner as a great composer, I bought a vocal score of Lohengrin: the only sample to be had at the Dublin music shops. The first few bars completely converted me.

This reminds me that when our household broke up and my mother went to London I suddenly found myself deprived of music, which had been my daily food all through my life. But the piano remained, though I had never touched it except to pick out a tune with one finger. In desperation I bought a technical handbook of music, containing a diagram of the keyboard. I then got out my mother's vocal score of Don Giovanni, and tried to play the overture. It took me some minutes to arrange my fingers on the notes of the first chord. What I suffered, what everybody in the house suffered, whilst I struggled on, laboring through arrangements of Beethoven's symphonies and vocal scores of all the operas and oratorios I knew, will never be told. In the end I learnt enough to thumb my way through anything. I never mastered the keyboard; but I did a good deal of rum-tum accompanying in my first days in London, and even once, in a desperate emergency, supplied the place of the absent half of the orchestra at a performance of Il Trovatore at a People's Entertainment evening at the Victoria Theatre in the Waterloo Road (the Old Vic) and came off without disaster, and in fact, mostly imposed my own *tempi* on the amiable and unassertive Italian conductor.

But this was outside my office life. My Hegira ended it in 1876.

6

END OF A CLERK IN DUBLIN

WHAT CHANGES A MAN
into a clerk, in Dublin or elsewhere? You cannot make a
Bedouin a clerk. But you can make an Englishman a clerk
quite easily. All you have to do is to drop him into a middle-
class family, with a father who cannot afford to keep him
nor afford to give him capital to start with, nor to carry his
education beyond reading, writing, and ciphering, but who
would feel disgraced if his son became a mechanic. Given
these circumstances, what can the poor wretch do but become a clerk?

I became a clerk myself. An uncle who, as a high official
in a Government department, had exceptional opportunities
of obliging people, not to mention obstructing them if he
disliked them, easily obtained for me a stool in a very genteel office; and I should have been there still if I had not
broken loose in defiance of all prudence, and become a professional man of genius. I am not one of those successful
men who can say "Why dont you do as I do?"

I sometimes dream that I am back in that office again, bothered by a consciousness that a long period has elapsed during which I have neglected my most important duties. I have drawn no money at the bank in the mornings, nor lodged any in the afternoons. I have paid no insurance premiums, nor head-rents, nor mortgage interests. Whole estates must have been sold up, widows and orphans left to starve, mortgages foreclosed, and the landed gentry of Ireland abandoned to general ruin, confusion, and anarchy, all through my unaccountable omission of my daily duties for years and years, during which, equally unaccountably, neither I nor anyone else in the office has aged by a single day. I generally wake in the act of asking my principals, with the authority which belongs to my later years, whether they realize what has happened, and whether they propose to leave so disgracefully untrustworthy a person as myself in a position of such responsibility.

In some ways I had a better time of it than most clerks. My associates in the office were apprentices of good social standing, mostly University men. I was not precluded from giving myself certain airs of being in the same position; and when, making a journey on the firm's business, I travelled first-class, my expenses were not challenged. But as it was assumed that I was a youth in training to be a man of business, I never got a living wage, though during most of that four and a half years I occupied a post of considerable responsibility. It had become vacant in an emergency when I was only a junior clerk. As it was of such a nature that it could not be left in abeyance even for half a day, I had been put into it as a stop-gap, and, like many another stop-gap, I stayed where I was stuck. Naturally, if I was to be tied to an office all day I preferred the higher post, the more varied work, the bigger responsibility. It was not a question of salary: I was quite prepared to take as big a salary as anybody would give me; but even had I been still at my starting figure of £18 a year, and been asked whether for that money I would act as junior clerk or senior partner, I should have unhesitatingly chosen to be senior partner. When, later in life, and active in the Socialist movement, I was posed with the usual assumption that inequality of work requires inequality of pay, I could answer from experience that, other things being equal, the higher the work the less people would do it for. If my employers had asked me to do the job of a charwoman they would have had to overcome my repugnance to it by a salary at least twenty times as large as they actually paid me after my promotion.

As my father had to make up the difference between what my employer paid me and what my subsistence cost, my employer was really sweating my father. He managed the estates of Irish landlords for them: a business in which agents got shot occasionally. Thus the industry which was feeding the country was exploited by the industry which was bleeding it to death. I speak without malice; for in the course of time I inherited an estate myself, and became an absentee Irish

63

landlord, agent and all. Accordingly I now maintain that landlordism is not always and necessarily bad: there were landlords even in Ireland who did more for their estates than their estates did for them. My wife's Irish estate cost her £600 a year until I induced her to sell it.

I left Ireland and escaped from clerking in 1876, when I was twenty. More than thirty years passed before I again set foot in my native town. A fancy took me to walk past the old office without being obliged to go into it. It happened that I had in my pocket a document which I had to attest before a Commissioner of Oaths. And as I passed the old door, I saw that there was on the first floor the office of such a commissioner. So I went in and mounted to the first floor. There I was received with distinguished consideration by the commissioner's clerk: a frockcoated gentleman of the utmost respectability and dignity. He regretted that his principal was out at the moment. We then had a friendly chat, in the course of which I said "Thirty years ago I was a clerk in the Estate Office downstairs."

Instantly his manner changed. With undisguised contempt and incredulity he said "I dont remember you."

I gasped. This man had been coming to the office every day during the thirty years in which I had wandered over the globe and changed from a nobody on an office stool to a celebrity with half a dozen reputations. And he seemed the happier man. Certainly he left me nowhere in point of self-esteem!

G.B.S., NEWLY TRANSPLANTED FROM DUBLIN TO LONDON

Immature, and apparently an arrant prig

MY NEWLY WED WIFE

7

NINE YEARS OF FAILURE AS NOVELIST ENDING IN SUCCESS AS CRITIC

BEHOLD ME, THEN, IN London in an impossible position. I was a foreigner—an Irishman—the most foreign of all foreigners when he has not gone through the British university mill. I was not, as I shall presently shew, uneducated; but what I knew was what the English university graduates did not know; and what they knew I either did not know or did not believe. I was provincial; I was opinionated; I had to change London's mind to gain any sort of acceptance or toleration.

London refused to tolerate me on any terms. I had one article accepted. It brought me fifteen shillings. A publisher shewed me some old blocks he had bought up. He wanted verses fitted to them for school prize books. I wrote a parody of the sort of thing he wanted, and sent it to him as a friendly joke. To my stupefaction, he thanked me and paid me five shillings. I was touched, and wrote him a serious verse for another picture. He took it as a joke in questionable taste; and my career as a versifier ended. Once I got a £5 job; but as it was not from a publisher or editor, but from a friendly lawyer who wanted a medical essay, evidently for use in an agitation concerning patent medicines, I was unable to follow up this success. Total, £6 in nine years. And yet I have been called an upstart.

In 1885 William Archer found me in the British Museum Reading Room, poring over Deville's French version of Karl Marx's Capital, with the orchestral score of Wagner's Tristan and Isolde beside it. He took my affairs in hand with such success that The Pall Mall Gazette, then still extant, sent me books to review; and the appointment of art critic to The World, which Archer was for the moment doubling with his regular function of dramatic critic, was transferred to me. I suddenly began to make money: £117 in the first year.

Archer, a Scot with family connexions which brought him a knowledge of the Norwegian language, was deeply under the spell of Ibsen; and he communicated the magic to me verbally. This and our anti-clerical views made a strong bond between us. Yet when he proposed that we should collaborate in writing a play of which he was to provide the plot and I the dialogue, his plot was "constructed" strictly on the then conventional lines.

Archer also proposed our collaboration in a drama he had planned in a most workmanlike manner on the technical lines of the "well made" constructed plays of Scribe and the French school. I took it in hand and produced two acts so defiant of these lines and unlike what Archer expected that he cried off; and my two acts languished for six or seven years, during which I read them to Henry Arthur Jones, then at the height of his vogue as a playwright. His comment was "Where's your murder?"

At last an Anglo-Dutch Ibsen enthusiast (Grein) started a coterie theatre called The Independent Theatre, and after a success-of-scandal with Ibsen, committed himself to the statement that there are in England hundreds of dramatic masterpieces unacted by the commercial theatres.

For this unsubstantiated guess I manufactured a scrap of evidence by fishing out my two acts; adding a third; and having them performed by Grein. Two performances were all he could afford. The first provoked a sensational mixture of applause and hooting, which I countered successfully in a speech before the curtain. A unanimously favorable reception of the second was followed by a press discussion of the play which lasted a fortnight. I was denounced as a pamphleteer void of dramatic faculty; but all the stage effects I had planned came off perfectly; and this was what convinced me that I was a born master of the theatre.

In 1888 The Star was founded; and on the advice of H. J. Massingham I was invited to join its political staff. But not one of my articles was considered printable. I proposed, as a compromise, that I should be allotted a column of the paper every week to fill with some non-political matter: say, music. This column, which was signed Corno di Bassetto (the Italian name of the basset horn), was a mixture of tomfoolery with genuine criticism. It was a success.

In 1890 the late Louis Engel, the best hated musical critic in Europe, and Archer's colleague on The World, got into a scrape, and had to leave the country. Archer instantly assured Edmund Yates, the editor, that Corno di Bassetto was Engel's only possible successor; and I left The Star, and, as G.B.S., wrote a page of The World on music every week until Yates's death in 1894, when I felt I must find another editor with the qualities of Yates: one not afraid of everything unusual, and aware how far he might safely venture in the novelty and heterodoxy which make criticism readable. So I resigned, and in 1895 accepted the post of theatre critic from Frank Harris, who had just become editor of The Saturday Review.

Harris had emigrated to America, where he had adventures as a cowboy, as a laborer employed in the building of Brooklyn Bridge, as a hotel manager, and as a lawyer. He had returned to England with the morals, manners, and conversation of a buccaneer, combined with a voice and elocution that gave him an imposing personal distinction and secured his acceptance at first sight into English professional and political society. But his love was for literature. He knew good writing from bad; and preferred good to bad. He was not afraid of heterodoxy, not indeed knowing that it was dangerous; for he believed himself to be a Christlike saint, and had no suspicion that in London he would have passed more easily as another Captain Kidd.

In short, the very man for me, and I the very man for him. Knowing that he would bully me if I did not first bully him in my own Irish fashion, I established the same footing with him as with Yates. We agreed for £6 a week. Yates had paid me £5. Not bad pay in those days.

The drama being a much less segregated cult than music, my fame at once increased with a rush; and thenceforth for years my name seldom appeared in print without the adjective brilliant, which I disliked, as it suggested a glittering superficiality which I abhorred. But I could not shake it off.

8

IN THE DAYS OF MY YOUTH

*From the late T. P. O'Connor's magazine entitled
M.A.P. (Mainly About People), the date of my
contribution being 17 September 1898.*

MY DEAR T. P.,

All autobiographies are lies. I do not mean unconscious,
unintentional lies: I mean deliberate lies. No man is bad
enough to tell the truth about himself during his lifetime,
involving, as it must, the truth about his family and his
friends and colleagues. And no man is good enough to tell
the truth to posterity in a document which he suppresses until
there is nobody left alive to contradict him.

I speak with the more confidence on the subject because
I have myself tried the experiment, within certain timid
limits, of being candidly autobiographical. But I have produced no permanent impression, because nobody has ever
believed me. I once told a fellow-critic [A. B. Walkley]
some facts about my family.

My paternal grandmother had fifteen children in the first twentytwo years of her marriage, and would perhaps have had fifteen more had her husband survived that experience. Of the fifteen she managed to bring up eleven, thus providing me with all but a dozen uncles and aunts and innumerable cousins on my father's side alone. My maternal grandfather married twice and had eight children, of whom only one died unmarried and childless.

Such families are rare nowadays; but in Ireland in the middle of the nineteenth century we thought nothing of them, ill as we could afford them. Like most fertile clans mine did not consist exclusively of teetotallers; nor did all its members remain until death up to the very moderate standard of legal sanity. One of them discovered a perfectly original method of suicide. It was simple to the verge of triteness; yet no human being had ever thought of it before. It was also amusing. But in the act of carrying it out my relative jammed the mechanism of his heart and died about a second before he succeeded in killing himself. The coroner's jury found that he died "from natural causes"; and the secret of the suicide was kept, not only from the public, but from most of the family.

I revealed that secret in private conversation to Walkley. He shrieked with laughter, and printed the whole story in his next *causerie*. It never for a moment occurred to him that it was true. Meanwhile, the extent to which I stood compromised with my relative's widow and brothers and sisters may be imagined.

Twice in my life I have given prosaically truthful instructions to solicitors, and been surprised to find that they were not carried out. They thought I must be romancing or joking.

If I were to attempt to write genuine autobiography here, the same difficulty would arise. I should give mortal offence to the few relatives who would know that I was writing the truth; and nobody else would believe me.

I am in the further difficulty that I have not yet ascertained the truth about myself. For instance, how far am I mad, and how far sane? I do not know. My specific talent has enabled me to cut a figure in my profession in London; but a man may, like Don Quixote, be clever enough to cut a figure, and yet be stark mad.

A critic recently described me as having "a kindly dislike of my fellow creatures." Dread would have been nearer the mark than dislike; for man is the only animal of which I am thoroughly and cravenly afraid. I have never thought much of the courage of a lion tamer. Inside the cage he is at least safe from other men. There is less harm in a well-fed lion. It has no ideals, no sect, no party, no nation, no class: in short, no reason for destroying anything it does not want to eat. In the Mexican war, the Americans burnt the Spanish fleet, and finally had to drag wounded men out of hulls which had become furnaces. The effect of this on one of the American commanders was to make him assemble his men

73

and tell them that he wished to declare before them that he believed in God Almighty. No lion would have done that. On reading it, and observing that the newspapers, representing normal public opinion, seemed to consider it a very creditable, natural, and impressively pious incident, I came to the conclusion that I must be mad. At all events, if I am sane, the rest of the world ought not to be at large. We cannot both see things as they really are.

My father was an Irish Protestant gentleman of the downstart race of younger sons. He had no inheritance, no profession, no manual skill, no qualification of any sort for any definite social function. He must have had some elementary education; for he could read and write and keep accounts more or less inaccurately; and he spoke and dressed like an Irish educated gentleman and not like a railway porter. But he certainly had not a university degree; and I never heard him speak of any school or college of which he could claim to be an alumnus. He had, however, been brought up to believe that there was an inborn virtue of gentility in all Shaws as partisans of William the Conqueror (the Dutch William of glorious pious and immortal memory, not the Norman adventurer) and owners of landed estates in Ireland or their relatives. Such younger sons as had outstanding ability made for Dublin, where one of them founded the Royal Bank, which old people in my boyhood still called Shaw's Bank. He was made a baronet, and founded the Dublin Shaws in a family seat called Bushy Park out Rathfarnham way. My father was a second cousin of the baronet, and was privileged to hire a carriage and attend the Bushy Park funerals, besides having a right to an invitation to certain family parties there. Necessarily all the Shaws were Protestants and snobs.

On the strength of his snobbery my father, after condescending to a clerkship or two, managed to assert his family claim on the State with sufficient success to obtain a post in the Four Courts (the Irish *Palais de Justice*). The post was abolished; and he was pensioned off. He sold the pension, and embarked with the proceeds in the corn trade, of which he had not the slightest knowledge; nor did he acquire much, as far as I can judge, to the day of his death. There was a mill a little way out in the country, which perhaps paid its own rent, since the machinery was kept in motion. But its chief use, I believe, was to amuse me and my two boon companions, the sons of my father's partner.

I believe Ireland, as far as the Protestant gentry is concerned, to be the most irreligious country in the world. I was christened by my uncle; and as my godfather was intoxicated and did not turn up, the sexton was ordered to promise and vow in his place, precisely as my uncle might have ordered him to put more coals on the vestry fire. I was never confirmed; and I believe my parents never were either. Of the seriousness with which English families took this rite I had no conception; for Irish Protestantism was not then a religion: it was a side in political faction, a class prejudice, a conviction that Roman Catholics are socially inferior persons who will go to hell when they die and leave Heaven in the exclusive possession of Protestant ladies and gentlemen. In my childhood I was sent every Sunday to a Sunday-school where genteel little children repeated texts, and were rewarded with cards inscribed with them. After an hour of this we were marched into the adjoining church (the Molyneux in Upper Leeson Street), to sit round the altar rails and fidget there until our neighbors must have wished the service over as heartily as we did. I suffered this, not for my salvation, but because my father's respectability demanded it. When we went to live in Dalkey we broke with the observance and never resumed it.

What helped to make "church" a hotbed of all the social vices was that no working folk ever came there. In England the clergy go among the poor, and sometimes do try desperately to get them to come to church. In Ireland the poor are Roman Catholics (Papists my Orange grandfather called them). The Protestant Church has nothing to do with them. I cannot say that in Ireland in my time there all the Protestants were the worse for what they called their religion. I can only answer for those I knew.

Imagine being taught to despise a workman, and to respect a gentleman, in a country where every rag of excuse for gentility is stripped off by poverty! Imagine being taught that there is one God, a Protestant and a perfect gentleman, keeping Heaven select for the gentry against an idolatrous impostor called the Pope! Imagine the pretensions of the English peerage on the incomes of the English middle class! I remember Stopford Brooke one day telling me that he discerned in my books an intense and contemptuous hatred for society. No wonder!

If I had not suffered from these things in my childhood, perhaps I could keep my temper about them. To an outsider there is nothing but comedy in the spectacle of a forlorn set of Protestant merchants in a Catholic country, led by a petty plutocracy of stockbrokers, doctors, and landagents, and camouflaged by that section of the landed gentry who, too heavily mortgaged to escape to London, play at being a Court and an aristocracy reigned over by a Vice-Regal exile persuaded to accept the post of Lord-Lieutenant at a salary of £20,000 a year, leaving him heavily out of pocket but making his wife a deputy queen. To such pretences, involving continual lying as to incomes and social standing, were sacrificed all the realities of life.

And now, what power did I find in Ireland religious enough to redeem me from this abomination of desolation? Quite simply, the power of Art. My mother, as it happened, had a considerable musical talent. In order to exercise it seriously, she had to associate with other people who had musical talent. My first doubt as to whether God could really be a good Protestant was suggested by the fact that the best voices available for combination with my mother's in the works of the great composers had been unaccountably vouchsafed to

77

Roman Catholics. Even the Divine gentility was presently called in question; for some of these vocalists were undeniably shopkeepers. If the best tenor, undeniably a Catholic, was at least an accountant, the buffo was a frank stationer.

There was no help for it: if my mother was to do anything but sing silly ballads in drawing rooms, she had to associate herself on an entirely unsectarian footing with people of like artistic gifts without the smallest reference to creed or class. She must actually permit herself to be approached by Roman Catholic priests, and at their invitation to enter that house of Belial, the Roman Catholic chapel, and sing the Masses of Mozart there. If religion is that which binds men to one another, and irreligion that which sunders, then must I testify that I found the religion of my country in its musical genius, and its irreligion in its churches and drawing rooms.

Let me add a word of gratitude to that cherished asylum of my boyhood, the National Gallery of Ireland. I believe I am the only Irishman who has ever been in it, except the officials. But I know that it did much more for me than the two confiscated medieval Cathedrals so magnificently "restored" out of the profits of the drink trade.

From Nature, too, one learns everywhere. She makes many an Irishman melancholy, and sets him snivelling about "the days that are over." Only the other day it was proposed to me that I should help to uplift my downtrodden country by assembling with other Irishmen to romance about 1798. I do not take the slightest interest in 1798. Until Irishmen apply themselves seriously to what the condition of Ireland is to be in 1998 they will get very little patriotism out of

yours sincerely,

G. BERNARD SHAW

London,
  1898

9

WHO I AM, AND WHAT I THINK

This catechism appeared in a shortlived magazine called The Candid Friend, in two instalments on May 11th and 18th 1901.

You ask me to tell you something of your parents and their influence on your life.

It is impossible to give you a Rougon-Macquart view of myself in less than twenty volumes. Let me tell you a story of my father. When I was a child, he gave me my first dip in the sea in Killiney Bay. He prefaced it by a very serious exhortation on the importance of learning to swim, culminating in these words "When I was a boy of only fourteen, my knowledge of swimming enabled me to save your Uncle Robert's life." Then, seeing that I was deeply impressed, he stooped, and added confidentially in my ear "and, to tell you the truth, I never was so sorry for anything in my life afterwards." He then plunged into the ocean, enjoyed a thoroughly refreshing swim, and chuckled all the way home.

Now I have never aimed consciously at anti-climax: it occurs naturally in my work. But there is no doubt some connection between my father's chuckling and the enjoyment produced in the theatre by my comedic methods.

When did you first feel inclined to write?

I never felt inclined to write, any more than to breathe. It never occurred to me that my literary sense was exceptional: I gave everyone credit for it; for there is nothing miraculous in a natural faculty to the man who has it. In art the amateur, the collector, the enthusiast, is the man who lacks the faculty for producing it. The Venetian wants to be a cavalry soldier; the Gaucho wants to be a sailor; the fish wants to fly and the bird to swim. I never wanted to write. I know now, of course, the scarcity of literary faculty; but I still dont want it. You cannot want a thing and have it, too.

What form did your literary work first take?

I vaguely remember that when I was a boy I concocted a short story and sent it to some boys' journal. It was about a man with a gun attacking another man in the Glen of the Downs. The gun was the centre of interest to me. My correspondence with Edward McNulty worked off my incipient literary energy.

I conducted one more long correspondence, this time with an English lady (Elinor Huddart) whose fervidly-imaginative novels would have made her known if I could have persuaded her to make her name public, or at least to stick to the same pen name, instead of changing it for every book. Virtually, my first works were the five novels I wrote from 1879 to 1883, which nobody would publish. I began a profane Passion Play, with the mother of the hero represented as a termagant, but never carried it through. I was always, fortunately for me, a failure as a trifler. All my attempts at Art for Art's Sake broke down: it was like hammering nails into sheets of note-paper.

You ask when I began to be interested in political questions and in what way they affected my work?

Well, you know how at the beginning of the eighties I heard an address by Henry George and how he opened my eyes to the importance of economics. I read Marx. Now the real secret of Marx's fascination was his appeal to an un-named, unrecognized passion: the hatred in the more gen-erous souls among the respectable and educated sections for the middle-class institutions that had starved, thwarted, mis-led, and corrupted them spiritually from their cradles. Marx's Capital is not a treatise on Socialism: it is a jeremiad against the bourgeoisie, supported by a mass of official evidence and a relentless Jewish genius for denunciation. It was addressed to the working classes; but the working man respects the bourgeoisie, and wants to be a bourgeois. It was the revolting sons of the bourgeoisie itself: Lassalle, Marx, Liebknecht, Morris, Hyndman, [add Lenin, Trotsky and Stalin]: all, like myself, bourgeois, who painted the flag red. Bakunin and Kropotkin, of the military and noble caste, were our extreme Anarchist Left. The professional and penniless younger son classes are the revolutionary element in society: the proletariat is the Conservative element, as Disraeli, the Tory Democrat, well knew. Marx made me a Socialist and saved me from becoming a literary man.

What was your first real success? Tell me how you felt about it. Did you ever despair of succeeding?

Never had any. Success, in that sense, is a thing that comes to you, and takes your breath away, as it came to Byron and Dickens and Kipling. What came to me was repeated failure. By the time I wore it down I knew too much to care about either failure or success.

Does poverty stand in the way of success or act as an incentive to it?

Poverty and lack of the leisure that only Socialism can give sterilizes most disastrously that small percentage of the population endowed by Providence with the capacity for thinking and managing without which Socialism is impossible.

But if you mean genteel impecuniosity, then all I can say is that our social system is so thoughtlessly arranged that it is impossible to say which is the greater obstruction to the development of a writer: money or the want of it. I could not undertake to rewrite The Pilgrim's Progress and Fors Clavigera as if Ruskin had been a tinsmith and Bunyan a gentleman of independent means. But whilst I am not sure

84

that want of money lames a poor man more than possession of it lames a rich one, I am quite sure that the class which has the pretensions and prejudices and habits of the rich without its money, and the poverty of the poor without the frankness to avow poverty: the people who dont go to the theatre because they cant afford the stalls and are ashamed to be seen in the gallery, are the worst-off of all. To be on the down grade from the zenith of *haute bourgeoisie* and landed gentry to the nadir at which the younger son's great-grandson gives up the struggle to keep up appearances, being no longer able to make £300 a year look like £800 in Ireland and Scotland nor £500 like £5000 in London; to be educated neither at the proletarian school and the Polytechnic nor at the University, but at some cheap private adventure academy for the sons of gentlemen; to exclude the poor from your visiting list and then find that the rest of the world excludes you: that is poverty at its most damnable. Yet a great deal of our literature and journalism has sprung from it. Think of the humiliation of the boy Dickens in the blacking ware-house, and his undying resentment of his mother's wanting him to stay there. Think of Trollope, at an upper-class school with holes in his trousers, because his father could not bring himself to dispense with a manservant. Ugh! Be a tramp or be a millionaire: it matters little which: what does matter is being a poor relation of the rich; and that is the very devil.

Communism came to my rescue. Though almost penniless I had a magnificent library in Bloomsbury, a priceless picture-gallery in Trafalgar Square, and another at Hampton Court, without any servants to look after or rent to pay. I had from Nature the brains to use them. As to professional music, I actually got paid later on for saturating myself with the best of it from London to Bayreuth. Friends! My visiting list has always been beyond price.

After all, what could I have bought with more than enough money for food, clothing, and lodging? Cigars? I dont smoke. Champagne? I dont drink. Thirty suits of fashionable clothes? The people I most avoid would ask me to dinner if I could be persuaded to wear such things. By this time I can afford them all; but I buy nothing I didnt buy before. Besides, I have an imagination. Ever since I can remember, I have only had to shut my eyes to be and do whatever I pleased. What are your trumpery Bond Street luxuries to me, George Bernard Sardanapalus? I exhausted romantic daydreaming before I was ten years old. Your popular novelists are now writing the stories I told to myself (and sometimes to others) before I replaced my first set of teeth.

Some day I will try to found a genuine psychology of fiction by writing down the history of my imagined life: duels, battles, love affairs with queens and all. The difficulty is that so much of it is too crudely erotic to be printable by an author of any delicacy. [When I wrote this in 1901, I did not believe that an author so utterly void of delicacy as Sigmund Freud could not only come into human existence, but become as famous and even instructive by his defect as a

blind man might by writing essays on painting, nor that the
ban could ever be lifted from the ponderous sex treatises of
Havelock Ellis.]

What do you think of journalism as a profession?

Daily journalism, being beyond mortal strength and endurance, trains literary men to scamp their work. A weekly
feuilleton is at least possible: I did one for ten years, taking
all the pains I was capable of to get to the bottom of every
sentence I wrote. There is an indescribable levity—not trivi-
ality, mind, but levity—something spritelike about the conclusions of the writer who will face the labor of digging
down to them. Half truths are congruous, heavy, serious, and
suggestive of a middle-aged or elderly philosopher. The fully
reasoned conclusion is often the first thing that comes into
the head of a fool or a child; and when a reasoner forces his
way to it through the many strata of his sophistications, it is
not only surprising but amusing.

Ten years of such work was an apprenticeship which made
me master of my profession. But it was not daily journalism.
I could not have achieved its quality had I undertaken more
than one feuilleton; and even that I could not have done without keeping myself up to the neck all the rest of the week
in other activities: gaining other efficencies and gorging myself with life and experience as well. My income as a journalist began in 1885 at £117. os. 3d.; and it ended at about
£500, by which time I had reached the age at which we

discover that journalism is a young man's standby, not an old man's livelihood. So, I conclude, even weekly journalism is superhuman except for young men. The older ones must scamp it; and the younger ones must live plainly and cheaply, if they are to get their authority up to the pitch at which they are allowed to say what they think. Of course, they do nothing of the sort. If they did, journalism would train them in literature as nothing else could. Would, but doesnt. It spoils them instead. If you want a problem stated, a practised journalist will do it with an air that is the next best thing to solving it. But he never solves it: he hasnt time, and wouldnt get paid any more for the solution if he had time. So he chalks up the statement, and runs away from the solution.

Were you always a vegetarian? How did you first become one?

No: I was a cannibal for twenty-five years. For the rest I have been a vegetarian. It was Shelley who first opened my eyes to the savagery of my diet; but it was not until 1880 or thereabouts that the establishment of vegetarian restaurants in London made a change practicable for me.

My vegetarianism has a quaint effect on my critics. You read an article purporting to be a review of my latest book, and discover that what the critic is really doing is defending his private life against mine, and that what you are reading is the *apologia pro sua vita* of a deeply-wounded man. The critic tries to go through his usual imposing pen performance;

but the blood of the Deptford Victualling Yard chokes him, and the horrible carcass groves of Farringdon Market rise up before him. All this *mauvaise honte* is the remorse of the meat-eater in the presence of the man who is a living proof that neither fish, flesh, nor fowl is indispensable to success in life and literature. All my other fads are familiar to them, and often shared by them. But this is a matter of blood-guilt; and *Blut ist ein ganz besondrer Saft.*

Does married life make a difference in your views?

What do you call married life? Real married life is the life of the youth and maiden who pluck a flower and bring down an avalanche on their shoulders. Thirty years of the work of Atlas; and then rest as pater and materfamilias. What can childless people with independent incomes, marrying at forty as I did, tell you about marriage? I know nothing about it except as a looker-on.

What is your honest opinion of G.B.S.?

Oh, one of the most successful of my fictions, but getting a bit tiresome, I should think. G.B.S. bores me except when he is saying something that needs saying and can best be said in the G.B.S. manner. G.B.S. is a humbug.

What is your definition of humor?

Anything that makes you laugh. But the finest sort draws a tear along with the laugh.

I want one word as to the meaning of the world-comedy from your point of view.

It is this thoughtless demand for a meaning that produces the comedy. You ask for it in one word though we are not within a million years, as yet, of seeing the world as it really is. We are intellectually still babies: this is perhaps why a baby's facial expression so strongly suggests the professional philosopher. All its mental energy is absorbed by its struggle to attain physical consciousness. It is learning to interpret the sensations of its eyes and ears and nose and tongue and finger-tips. It is ridiculously delighted by a silly toy, absurdly terri-fied by a harmless bogey. Well, we are all still as much babies in the world of thought as we were in our second year in the world of sense. Men are not real men to us: they are heroes and villains, respectable persons and criminals. Their qualities are virtues and vices; the natural laws that govern them are gods and devils; their destinies are rewards and ex-piations; their reasoning a formula of cause and effect with the horse mostly behind the cart. They come to me with their heads full of these figments, which they call, if you please, "the world," and ask me what is the meaning of them, as if I or anyone else were God Omniscient and could tell them. Pretty funny this: eh? But when they ostracize, punish, mur-der, and make war to impose by force their grotesque religions and hideous criminal codes, then the comedy becomes a tragedy. The Army, the Navy, the Church, the Bar, the theatres, the picture-galleries, the libraries, and the trade unions are forced to bolster up their pet hallucinations. Enough. You expect me to prate about the Absolute, about Reality, about The First Cause, and to answer the universal Why. When I see these words in print the book goes into the basket. Good morning.

London,
  1901

10

HOW I BECAME A PUBLIC SPEAKER

IN THE WINTER OF 1879,
James Lecky, exchequer clerk from Ireland, and privately
interested in phonetics, keyboard temperament, and Gaelic,
all of which subjects he imposed on me, dragged me to a
meeting of a debating society called The Zetetical: a junior
copy of the once well known Dialectical Society founded to
discuss John Stuart Mill's Essay on Liberty when that was
new. Both societies were strongly Millite. In both there was
complete freedom of discussion, political, religious, and sexual.
Women took an important part in the debates, a special feature of which was that each speaker, at the conclusion of his
speech, could be cross-examined on it. The tone was strongly
individualistic, atheistic, Malthusian, Ingersollian, Darwinian,
and Herbert Spencerian. Huxley, Tyndall, and George Eliot
were on the shelves of all the members. Championship of
the Married Women's Property Act had hardly been silenced
even by the Act itself. Indignation at prosecutions for blasphemous libel was *de rigueur;* and no words were too strong

for invective against such leading cases as those of Annie Besant and Shelley, whose children were torn from them by the Lord Chancellor because, as professed atheists, they were presumed to be unfit for parentage. Socialism was regarded as an exploded fallacy of Robert Owen's; and nobody dreamt that within five years Marxist Socialism would snatch away all the younger generation, and sweep the Dialectical and Zetetical Societies into the blind cave of eternal night. Cobdenist individualism in industry was fundamental.

When I went with Lecky to the Zetetical meeting I had never spoken in public. I knew nothing about public meetings or their order. I had an air of impudence, but was really an arrant coward, nervous and self-conscious to a heartbreaking degree. Yet I could not hold my tongue. I started up and said something in the debate, and then, feeling that I had made a fool of myself, as in fact I had, I was so ashamed that I vowed I would join the Society; go every week; speak in every debate; and become a speaker or perish in the attempt. I carried out this resolution. I suffered agonies that no one suspected. During the speech of the debater I resolved to follow, my heart used to beat as painfully as a recruit's going under fire for the first time. I could not use notes: when I looked at the paper in my hand I could not collect myself enough to decipher a word. And of the four or five points that were my pretext for this ghastly practice I invariably forgot the best.

The Society must have hated me; for to it I seemed so

uppish and self-possessed that at my third meeting I was asked to take the chair. I consented as offhandedly as if I were the Speaker of the House of Commons; and the secretary probably got his first inkling of my hidden terror by seeing that my hand shook so that I could hardly sign the minutes of the previous meeting. My speeches must have been little less dreaded by the Society than they were by myself; but I noticed that they were hardly ever ignored; for the speaker of the evening, in replying, usually addressed himself almost exclusively to my remarks, seldom in an appreciative vein. Besides, though ignorant of economics, I had read, in my boyhood, Mill on Liberty, on Representative Government, and on the Irish Land Question; and I was as full of Darwin, Tyndall, and George Eliot as most of my audience. Yet every subject struck my mind at an angle that produced reflections new to my audience. My first success was when the Society paid to Art, of which it was utterly ignorant, the tribute of setting aside an evening for a paper on it by a lady in the esthetic dress momentarily fashionable in Morrisan cliques just then. I wiped the floor with that meeting; and several members confessed to me afterwards that it was this performance that first made them reconsider their first impression of me as a bumptious discordant idiot.

I persevered doggedly. I haunted all the meetings in London where debates followed lectures. I spoke in the streets, in the parks, at demonstrations, anywhere and everywhere possible. In short, I infested public meetings like an officer afflicted with cowardice, who takes every opportunity of going under fire to get over it and learn his business.

I had quiet literary evenings in University College at the meetings of the New Shakespear Society under F. J. Furnivall, and breezier ones at his Browning Society, reputedly an assembly of longhaired esthetes, but really a conventicle where evangelistic elderly ladies discussed their religion with Furnivall, who, being what was called a Muscular Christian (slang for sporting parson), could not forgive Jesus for not putting up a fight in Gethsemane. When he founded a Shelley Society I joined, and at its first public meeting proclaimed myself, like Shelley, a Socialist, Atheist, and Vegetarian. Two Browningite ladies resigned on the spot.

I joined another very interesting debating society called the Bedford, founded by Stopford Brooke, who had not then given up his pastorate at Bedford Chapel to devote himself to literature.

At all these meetings I took part in the debates. My excessive nervousness soon wore off. One of the public meetings I haunted was at the Nonconformist Memorial Hall in Farringdon Street in 1884. The speaker of the evening, very handsome and eloquent, was Henry George, American apostle of Land Nationalization and Single Tax. He struck me dumb and shunted me from barren agnostic controversy to economics. I read his Progress and Poverty, and went to a meeting of Hyndman's Marxist Democratic Federation, where I rose and protested against its drawing a red herring across

96

G.B.S., PLATFORM SPELLBINDER

Portrait by Bertha Newcombe, spellbound.

SINGING AND PLAYING

the trail blazed by George. I was contemptuously dismissed as a novice who had not read the great first volume of Marx's Capital.

I promptly read it, and returned to announce my complete conversion by it. Immediately contempt changed to awe; for Hyndman's disciples had not read the book themselves, it being then accessible only in Deville's French version in the British Museum reading room, my daily resort. From that hour I was a speaker with a gospel, no longer only an apprentice trying to master the art of public speaking.

I at once applied for membership of the Democratic Federation, but withdrew my application on discovering the newly founded Fabian Society, in which I recognized a more appropriate *milieu* as a body of educated middle-class intelligentsia: my own class in fact. Hyndman's congregation of manual-working pseudo-Marxists could for me be only hindrances.

After my conversion I soon became sufficiently known as a Socialist orator to have no further need to seek out public debates: I was myself sought after. This began when I accepted an invitation from a Radical Club at Woolwich to lecture to it. At first I thought of reading a written lecture; for it seemed hardly possible to speak for an hour without text when I had hitherto spoken for ten minutes or so only in debates. But if I were to lecture formally on Socialism for an hour, writing would be impossible for want of time: I must extemporize. The lecture was called Thieves, and was a demonstration that the proprietor of an unearned income inflicted on the community exactly the same injury as a burglar does. I spoke for an hour easily, and from that time always extemporized.

This went on for about twelve years, during which I sermonized on Socialism at least three times a fortnight average. I preached whenever and wherever I was asked. It was first come first served with me: when I got an application for a lecture I gave the applicant the first date I had vacant, whether it was for a street corner, a public-house parlor, a market place, the economic section of the British Association, the City Temple, a cellar or a drawing room. My audiences varied from tens to thousands. I expected opposition but got hardly any. Twice, in difficulties raised by attempts of the police to stop Socialist street meetings (they always failed in the end because the religious sects, equally active in the open air, helped the Socialists to resist them), I was within an ace of going to prison. The first time was in Dodd Street in dockland, where the police capitulated on the morning of the day when I volunteered to defy them. The second time, many years later at the World's End in Chelsea, a member of a rival Socialist Society disputed the martyr's palm with me, and, on a division, defeated me by two votes, to my secret relief. My longest oration lasted four hours in the open air on a Sunday morning to crowds at Trafford Bridge in Manchester. One of my best speeches was delivered in Hyde Park in torrents of rain to six policemen sent to watch me, plus only the secretary of the Society that had asked me to speak, who held an umbrella over me. I made up my mind to interest those policemen, though as they were on duty to listen to me, their usual practice, after being convinced that I was harmless, was to pay no further attention. I entertained them for more than an hour. I can still see their waterproof capes shining in the rain when I shut my eyes.

I never took payment for speaking. It often happened that provincial Sunday Societies offered me the usual ten guinea fee to give the usual sort of lecture, avoiding controversial politics and religion. I always replied that I never lectured on anything but very controversial politics and religion, and that my fee was the price of my railway ticket third class if the place was further off than I could afford to go at my own expense. The Sunday Society would then assure me that on these terms I might lecture on anything I liked and how I liked. Occasionally, to avoid embarrassing other lecturers who lived by lecturing, the account was settled by a debit and credit entry: that is, I was credited with the usual fee and expenses, and gave it back as a donation to the Society. In this way I secured perfect freedom of speech, and was armed against the accusation of being a professional agitator. For instance, at the election in 1892, I was making a speech in the Town Hall of Dover when a man rose and shouted to the audience not to let itself be talked to by a hired professional agitator from London. I immediately offered to sell him my emoluments for £5. He hesitated; and I came down to £4. I offered to make it five shillings—half-a-crown—a shilling—sixpence. When he would not deal even at a penny I claimed that he must know perfectly well that I was there at my own expense. If I had not been able to do this, the meeting, which was a difficult and hostile one (Dover being then a notoriously corrupt constituency), would probably have broken up.

How necessary was this entirely voluntary position I learnt from a professional speaker who was hired at £3 a week to follow me to all my meetings and confute me by the Duke of Argyll's Liberty & Property Defence League. Travelling together we soon became pleasant acquaintances. He always made the same speech and I always made the same smashing reply. When his League broke up he offered his services to the Fabian Society, and was amazed to learn that Fabian speakers were unpaid, and that I had actually been lecturing "for nothing."

Once, in St James's Hall, London, at a meeting in favor of Women's Suffrage, I ventured on a curious trick with success. Just before I spoke, a hostile contingent entered the room; and I saw that we were outnumbered, and that an amendment would be carried against us. The intruders were all Socialists of the anti-Fabian persuasion, led by a man whom I knew very well, and who was at that time excitable almost to frenzy, worn out with public agitation and private worries. It occurred to me that if, instead of carrying an amendment, they could be goaded to break up the meeting and disgrace themselves, the honors would remain with us. I made a speech that would have made a bishop swear or a sheep fight. The leader, stung beyond endurance, dashed madly to the platform to answer me. His followers, thinking he was leading a charge, instantly stormed the platform; broke up the meeting; and reconstituted it with their leader as chairman. I then demanded a hearing, which was duly granted me as a matter of fair play; and I had another innings with great satisfaction to myself. No harm was done, nor any blow struck; but the papers next morning described a scene of violence and destruction that left nothing to be desired by the most sanguinary schoolboy.

I never challenged anyone to debate publicly with me. It seemed to me an unfair practice for a seasoned public speaker to challenge a comparative novice to a duel with tongues, of no more value than any other sort of duel. But I now regret that when I was myself still a novice, a debate between me and Charles Bradlaugh which the Socialist League (Morris's body) tried to arrange did not come off. Bradlaugh was a heroic fighting platform thunderer; and I should have been only a light weight trying to outbox a heavy one who had won in all his conflicts; but I could at least have said my say. The Socialist League challenged him to debate, and chose me as their champion, though I was not a member. I was frightened, but could not back out. Bradlaugh, however, made it a condition that I should be bound by all the pamphlets and utterances of the Social-Democratic Federation, a strongly anti-Fabian body. Of course I should have let him make what conditions he pleased, and paid no further attention to them. But I was too green to see this. I proposed simply: "Will Socialism benefit the English people?" He would accept this only on condition that Socialism was to mean what Hyndman's Federation meant. I refused to be bound thus; and the debate—as I think he must have intended—did not come off, rather to my relief; for I was very doubtful of being able to make any show against him. I have never quite forgiven myself for this missed opportunity; but it was less cowardice than diffidence, with which in those early days I was still much afflicted. I was really a better speaker and a more formidable antagonist than I knew. I had already faced Bradlaugh on his own ground at the Hall of Science in the City Road. My seat was far back; and when I rose I had hardly uttered two sentences when Bradlaugh started up and said: "The gentleman is a speaker. Come to the platform," which I accordingly did through much curious staring. Bradlaugh devoted almost all his reply to my speech. He evidently thought more of me than I did of myself; and it pleases me to imagine that he refused a set debate with me much as Edmund Kean refused to act with Macready.

Later on he debated the Eight Hour Day with Hyndman, whom he was confident he could pulverize. Neither of them stuck to the subject; and the result was so inconclusive that both sides were dissatisfied; and it was arranged that the

question should be re-debated by me with the late G. V.
Foote, Bradlaugh's successor in the Presidency of the National
Secular Society, and a firstrate speaker. In the Hall of Science
we went at it hammer-and-tongs for two nights. Oratorically
honors were even; but I was more at home in economics than
Foote, and should, I believe, have won the verdict had a
vote been taken. The debate was reported in a booklet published by George Standring.

My public speaking brought me a very necessary qualification for political work: the committee habit. Whatever Society
I joined I was immediately placed on the executive committee.
At first I did what authors usually do in their Bohemian
anarchism and individualism. When they are defeated on
any issue they resign. I did this when the Land Restoration
League refused to add Socialism to its program on my sug-
gestion. I never did it again. I soon learnt the rule Never
Resign. I learnt also that committees of agitators are always
unanimous in the conviction that Something Must Be Done,
but very vague as to what. They talk and talk and can come
to no conclusion. The member who has something definite
to propose, and who keeps it up his sleeve until the rest are
completely bothered, is then master of the situation even
when nobody quite agrees with him. It is that or nothing;
and Something Must Be Done. This is how a man in a
minority of one becomes a leader. I was often in a minority
of one.

How lack of committee training and platform technique

disables even the most gifted thinkers was illustrated by the case of H. G. Wells, with whom I had a famous debate when he tried to capture the Fabian Society at one blow. As a speaker and committee man I had the advantage of him by ten years, whilst he was a complete novice. To say that I annihilated him is nothing: he saved me the trouble by annihilating himself. He could only misbehave himself. Fortunately for him he did this so outrageously that the Society very sensibly saw through the situation, and, whilst dismissing him as tactically impossible, thought none the worse of him as a Socialist pioneer, and none the better of me for my superiority as a platform artist.

I must not leave incipient orators to suppose that my technique as a speaker was acquired by practice alone. Practice only cured my nervousness, and accustomed me to speak to multitudes as well as to private persons. I have elsewhere described how I became acquainted with old Richard Deck, superannuated Alsatian *basso profundo* opera singer, who believed he had discovered a new method of *bel canto,* and imagined that he could not only renew his career as a singer when he had fully mastered it, but also regenerate civilization with it. He died destitute in University College Hospital. Meanwhile, however, being a pupil of Delsarte, he taught me that to be intelligible in public the speaker must relearn the alphabet with every consonant separately and explosively articulated, and foreign vowels distinguished from British diphthongs. Accordingly I practised the alphabet as a singer practises scales until I was in no danger of saying "Loheerye-lentheethisharpointed sword" instead of "Lo here *I* l*e*nd *th*ee *thiss sh*ar*p po*inted sword," nor imagine that when imitating the broadest dialects articulation is less to be studied than in classical declamation. Lessons in elocution should always be taken by public speakers when a phonetically competent teacher is available. But art must conceal its artificiality; and the old actor who professes to teach acting, and knows nothing of phonetic speech training, is to be avoided like the plague.

At last I could not deal with all the invitations I received. And the repetition of the same figures and arguments became tiresome: I was in danger of becoming a windbag with only one speech. I had seen too much of the fate of Trade Union organizers who, beginning as teetotallers, were forced by the need for "stoking up" their fresh audiences with the same stale speech to stoke themselves up by drinking. By 1895 I was no longer in full blast; and a breakdown of my health, followed by my marriage in 1898, finished me as a Sunday platform star. Thenceforth I orated on special occasions only, or at Fabian public meetings and in the St Pancras Borough Council, to which I got elected while it was still a Vestry. But I did not forget my acquired technique as a platform artist. It lasted until my final retirement from personal performances in 1941: my eightyfifth year.

11

FRUITFUL FRIENDSHIPS

A FEW WEEKS AFTER I joined the Zetetical Society I was much struck by a speaker who appeared once and took part in the debate. He was about 21, rather below middle height, with small hands and feet, and a profile that suggested an improvement on Napoleon the Third, his nose and imperial moustache being of that shape. He had a fine forehead, a long head, eyes that were built on top of two highly developed organs of speech (according to the phrenologists), and remarkably thick, strong, dark hair. He knew all about the subject of debate; knew more than the lecturer; knew more than anybody present; had read everything that had ever been written; and remembered all the facts that bore on the subject. He used notes, read them, ticked them off one by one, threw them away, and finished with a coolness and clearness that seemed to me miraculous.

This was the ablest man in England: Sidney Webb. Quite the wisest thing I ever did was to force my friendship on him and to keep it; for from that time I was not merely a futile Shaw but a committee of Webb and Shaw.

Webb, later Baron Passfield of Passfield Corner, now buried in Westminster Abbey at my urgent demand, proved one of the most extraordinary and capable of world-bettering administrators and historians. I somehow divined this whilst we were still both nobodies. As a disciple of John Stuart Mill he had grasped the economic certainty that private property in the sources of production plus freedom of contract must produce a plutocracy face to face with a proletariat, and substitute class war for genuine democracy. Adam Smith, Malthus and Ricardo, Austin and Macaulay, knew this, but saw no alternative. Webb, as a modern upper division civil servant, knew that there is a quite feasible corrective alternative in nationalization of the sources of production, and direct management of vital industries by the State, of the existence and success of which he had at his fingers' ends an overwhelming list of examples. On this basis he was a convinced Socialist.

The difference between Shaw with Webb's brains, knowledge, and official experience and Shaw by himself was enormous. But as I was and am an incorrigible histrionic mountebank, and Webb was the simplest of geniuses, I was often in the centre of the stage whilst he was invisible in the prompter's box.

My conversion to economics by Henry George brought me into contact with a Georgite body called The Land Reform

Union, which survived for some years as The English Land Restoration League. Here I met James Leigh Joynes, an Eton master, Sydney Olivier, and Henry Hyde Champion, besides some Christian Socialist clergymen including Stewart Headlam, Symes of Nottingham, with Sarson and Shuttleworth, who were organized as The Guild of St Matthew. Symes, I remember, argued that Land Nationalization would settle everything, to which I replied that if capital were still privately appropriated, Symes would remain "the chaplain of a pirate ship." Sarson, on the strength of the First Article of the Church of England, held that Anglicanism was atheistic. He became known as Cecil Sharp's colleague in their collection of Somerset folk songs.

Now Joynes was a vegetarian, a humanitarian, a Shelleyan. He was deprived of his Eton post because he made a tour in Ireland with Henry George, and was arrested with him by the police, who supposed the two to be emissaries of the Clan na Gael. Joynes's sister was married to an Eton house master, Henry Salt. Salt was also a vegetarian, a humanitarian, a Shelleyan, a De Quinceyite. He loathed Eton housekeeping. As soon as he had saved enough to live in a laborer's cottage in the country (he had no children) he threw up his house; shook the dust of Eton from his feet; and founded a Humanitarian League. He and I and his wife, Kate Salt, with whom I used to play duets on the noisiest grand piano that ever descended from Eton to a Surrey cottage, became very close friends. My article headed A Sunday in the Surrey Hills in

The Pall Mall Gazette describes my first visit to them in the country; and several scenes of my Plays Pleasant and Unpleasant were written in the heather during my visits to them. Here you have the link between me and the Humanitarians. Intimate in the Salt household was Edward Carpenter. We called him the Noble Savage. He also played duets with Kate, and induced me to wear sandals, which I discarded after my first long walk in them ended with bleeding feet.

In this circle there was no question of Henry George and Karl Marx, but a good deal of Walt Whitman and Thoreau. The worst that happened was the death of Joynes, who, having a disordered heart, was slaughtered by medical immobilization and alcoholic stimulation: a treatment so grossly and obviously lethal that I have never forgiven the medical profession for it. It is still in vogue. He left a volume of excellent translations of the revolutionary songs of the German revolutionists of 1848. Salt published several monographs on Shelley, James Thompson, Jefferies, and De Quincey. He ended with Eton reminiscences and a translation of Virgil. He entitled his autobiography Seventy Years Among Savages.

Now back for a moment to the Land Reform Union. I met Sydney Olivier there. He was an upper division clerk in the Colonial Office. So was Sidney Webb. He and Webb were the two resident clerks, very close friends. When the Fabian Society was founded in 1884, I was attracted by its name and its tract called Why Are The Many Poor? I persuaded Webb to join, Marx having convinced me that what the movement needed was not Hegelian theorizing but an unveiling of the official facts of Capitalist civilization, which Webb had at his fingers' ends. His first contribution, a tract called Facts for Socialists, was the effective beginning of Fabianism.

Olivier, who died a peer in 1943, combined firstrate administrative ability with unfailing goodwill and a complete autocratic absence of any other sort of conscience. I have described him in my contribution to his biography. He had made friends at Oxford with Graham Wallas, who afterwards joined us. For some years the leaders in the Politbureau or Thinking Cabinet of the Fabian policy were Webb, Olivier, Wallas, Shaw, and the Tory Democrat Hubert Bland.

As my colleagues were men of exceptional character and attainments, I was soon able to write with a Fabian purview and knowledge which made my feuilletons and other literary performances quite unlike anything that the ordinary literary hermit-crab could produce. Thus the reputedly brilliant extraordinary Shaw was in fact brilliant and extraordinary because he had in the Fabian Politbureau an incomparable critical threshing machine for his ideas. When I seemed most original and fantastic, I was often simply an amanuensis and a mouthpiece with a rather exceptional literary and dramatic knack, cultivated by dogged practice.

My colleagues knocked much nonsense, ignorance, and vulgar provinciality out of me; for we were on quite ruthless critical terms with one another.

In the Fabian Cabinet, however, there was considerable

strife of temperaments; and in the other Socialist societies splits and schisms were frequent; for the English are very quarrelsome. I believe that some of my own usefulness lay in smoothing out these frictions by an Irish sort of tact which in England seemed the most outrageous want of it. Whenever there was a quarrel I betrayed everybody's confidence by analyzing it and stating it lucidly in the most exaggerated terms. Result: both sides agreed that it was all my fault. I was denounced on all hands as a reckless mischiefmaker, but forgiven as a privileged Irish lunatic.

I flatter myself that the unique survival of the Fabian Society among the forgotten wrecks of its rivals, all very contemptuous of it, was due not only to its policy, but in its early days to the one Irish element in its management.

So much for the Fabian friendships that went to the making of G.B.S. the brilliant.

Photo by "P. C.," Dublin

TORCA COTTAGE: MY NATURE SCHOOL

"THE MEN OF IRELAND ARE MORTAL AND
TEMPORAL, BUT HER HILLS ARE ETERNAL."
G.B.S.

TORCA COTTAGE
THE HOME OF
GEORGE BERNARD SHAW
FROM 1866 TO 1874

ERECTED BY THE DALKEY DEVELOPMENT
AND PROTECTION ASSOCIATION 1947.

THE PLAQUE

12

AM I AN EDUCATED PERSON?

I CANNOT TOO OFTEN repeat that though I have no academic qualifications I am in fact much more highly educated than most university scholars. My home was a musical one; and the music was the "learned" music that began for me with Handel, and the dramatic music that began with Gluck and Mozart, the two constituting a body of modern cultural art to which the literature of the dead languages can make no pretension except in the great translations of Gilbert Murray, which are as English and as modern as any original works in our tongue, and remind us that Shakespear also was a translator and transfigurer of old stories and not their first inventor. My family, though kindly, might be called loveless; but what did that matter to a child who could sing *A te O cara* and *Suone la tromba intrepida* before he was perfect in the Church Catechism. In these there was sentiment and chivalry enough for any child.

This education has never ceased. It has gone on from Rossini, Meyerbeer, and Verdi to Wagner, from Beethoven to Sibelius, from British dilutions of Handel and Mendelssohn to the genuine English music of Elgar and Vaughan Williams and from the wholetone mode of Debussy and the chromatic mode of Schonberg to the experiments of Cyril Scott in the technical chaos which ensued when the forbidden consecutives and unprepared unresolved discords and "false relations" of the old textbooks became the latest fashion. Much of it has proved the soundness of Oscar Wilde's precept "Avoid the latest fashion or you will be hopelessly out of date in six months." When Wagner trumpeted unprepared major ninths at us in Tannhäuser, we stopped our ears. He went on to do the same with thirteenths. They startle nobody nowadays; but they certainly startled me, who could remember being impressed as by something tremendous when I first heard Beethoven's youthful Prometheus Overture open with an unprepared diminished seventh with the seventh in the bass.

How is this for textbook jargon? Can any university graduate who has had Virgil and Homer, Horace and Juvenal, rubbed mercilessly into him at Eton, Harrow, Winchester, or Rugby, beat it? Is the involution of the pattern verse of John Gilpin and The Ancient Mariner into the unmeasured wamblings now printed to look like poetry more educative than the evolution from decorative dance music to the mood-expressing music of Beethoven, bridged by Mozart's miraculous gift for combining the two?

114

I shall be reminded that there are university musicians: Doctors of Music like Stanford and Parry. But the effect of such degrees is to make their holders believe that they are composing when they are only covering music paper with imitations of outmoded composers, disparaging meanwhile masters like Bach and Elgar, neither of whom ever had a lesson in thoroughbass. My governess taught me my alphabet; but nobody taught me to write my plays, which were denounced as no plays until they made so much money that the fashion changed, and I was hailed successor to Shakespear.

Personal experience of contemporary developments in art is far more instructive than any study of ancient documents can be. No memorizing examinee can feel the development from Aeschylus to Euripides and its *dégringolade* to Menander as I felt the development from Donizetti to Wagner, from Bouguereau to Gauguin, from Leader to Wilson Steer and Monet, from Canova to Rodin, from Scribe and Sardou to Ibsen, from Barry Sullivan to Irving, from Colenso to Inge, from Tennyson to Browning, from Macaulay to Marx, from Max Weismann to Herbert Dingle, from Tyndall to Clerk-Maxwell, Planck, and Einstein, and from Kingdom Clifford to Hardy: in short, from adoring rehearings of the masterpieces of the dead to the pressures on my living self of startling departures that were new to me.

Academic educational tests are better than none. Whoever has studied the steps from Aristotle to Lucretius, from Plato-cum-Socrates to Plotinus, Thucydides to Gibbon, Ptolemy to

Copernicus, Saint Peter to Robert Owen, Aquinas to Hus and Luther, Erasmus to Voltaire, can at least find out what was done last time and give certificates to those who can do it again. But without living experiences no person is educated. With nothing but academic degrees, even when overloaded by a smattering of dead languages and twopennorth of algebra, the most erudite graduates may be noodles and ignoramuses. The vital difference between reading and experience is not measurable by examination marks. On the strength of that difference I claim arrogantly to be one of the best educated men in the world, and on occasion have dismissed 95 per cent. of the academic celebrities, with all due respect for the specific talents enjoyed by a few of them, as nitwits.

It was this equipment that saved me from being starved out of literature. When William Archer delegated to me a job as a critic of painting which had been pushed on him, and for which he was quite unqualified, I rose like a rocket. My weekly feuilletons on all the fine arts in succession are still readable after sixty years. All that the exhibitions and performances that London could provide were open freely to me throughout the decade that followed my unanimous rebuffs as novelist. The better my novels the more they revolted the publishers' professional readers; but as a critic I came to the top irresistibly, whilst contemporary well-schooled literary beginners, brought up in artless British homes, could make no such mark.

These years of criticism advanced my mental education by

compelling me to deliver carefully considered judgments, and to discriminate between the brilliant talents and technical accomplishments of the fashionable celebrities whose vogue ended with their deaths or sooner, and the genius that is not for an age but for all time. I heard beginners who, fresh from their teachers' coaching, gave the most promising displays. But not knowing the value of what they had been taught, they collapsed into commonplace when they escaped from tutelage. Only from such experiences can a critic become skilled in analysis, and learn that the critic who cannot analyze is easily duped.

I am still learning in my ninetysecond year.

As to languages and mathematics, my qualifications are negligible. I can read French as familiarly as English; and in Italy and Spain I can gather the news from the local papers. I know enough German to guess my way through most of the letters I receive in that language. As a linguist in conversation I am hopeless. As to mathematics I have the arithmetic (now very fallible) of an ex-cashier; but higher mathematics I can only comprehend and imagine without the smallest expertness. Technically I am a duffer; but in my day, measured by its yardsticks, I seemed an Admirable Crichton.

Great as is my debt to famous books, great pictures, and noble music for my education I should be even more ignorant than I am but for my removal at the age of ten from the street in which I was born, half of it faced with a very unpicturesque field which was soon obscured by a hoarding plastered with advertisements, to Torca Cottage, high on Dalkey Hill, commanding views of Dublin Bay from Dalkey Island to Howth Head and of Killiney Bay from the island to Bray Head, with a vast and ever changing expanse of sea and sky far below and far above.

Happiness is never my aim. Like Einstein I am not happy and do not want to be happy: I have neither time nor taste for such comas, attainable at the price of a pipeful of opium or a glass of whiskey, though I have experienced a very superior quality of it two or three times in dreams. But I had one moment of ecstatic happiness in my childhood when my mother told me that we were going to live in Dalkey. I had only to open my eyes there to see such pictures as no painter could make for me. I could not believe that such skies existed anywhere else in the world until I read Shakespear's "this majestical roof fretted with golden fire," and wondered where he could have seen it if not from Torca Cottage.

The joy of it has remained with me all my life.

Ayot Saint Lawrence,
  3rd August 1947

13

WHAT IS MY RELIGIOUS FAITH?

I AM BY INFANT BAP-
tism a member of the Protestant Episcopal Church of Ireland; but I cannot believe more than two tenets of its creed, and these (the Communion of Saints and the Life Everlasting) only in an entirely unconventional sense, nor in its Thirtynine Articles, which, compiled for the sake of political peace and quietness to face both ways between Roman Catholicism and Puritanism, are too self-contradictory to be accepted by anyone capable of consecutive thinking. Its other creed, the Athanasian, much objected to by the Broad Churchmen of my time because they thought its damnatory clause implied a belief in a brimstone hell, against which they were in full revolt, I endorse, because I interpret it as meaning that understanding and not faith is what the world most needs, and that people not subtle enough to accept its apparent paradoxes as valid statements of biological fact may be rhetorically described as intellectually damned.

Such scepticisms would make me chargeable with apostasy

under what is called the Blasphemy Law if I had ever been confirmed; but as I was not, I shall plead, if indicted, that the charge lies against my godfathers and godmothers (they are all dead) and not against myself.

This leaves me open to the question "If you are not a Protestant Churchman, what are you?"

At first I used to reply that I was an Atheist. But this was no answer; for what sensible people need to know is what people believe, not what they dont believe. At that time, however, professed Atheists, unless also plutocrats, were being savagely persecuted. Bradlaugh was thrown out of the House of Commons with such violence that John Bright, who arrived just in time to see him dragged down the stairs by six policemen, was horrified. His successor as head of the National Secular Society, G. W. Foote, was imprisoned for a year for publishing a picture of Samuel anointing Saul in modern clothes. It was a point of honor for their fellow-apostates to give them emphatic and unqualified support by professing themselves either Atheists or Agnostics. I preferred to call myself an Atheist because belief in God then meant belief in the old tribal idol called Jehovah; and I would not, by calling myself an Agnostic, pretend that I did not know whether it existed or not. I still, when I am dealing with old-fashioned Fundamentalists, tell them that as I do not believe in this idol of theirs they may as well write me off as, for their purposes, an Atheist.

What, then, was I? When G. W. Foote became insolvent

and his petition in bankruptcy raised the question of who was to succeed him if he had to resign his presidency of the National Secular Society, some of the members, headed by George Standring, placed me on a list of possibles, and invited me to address the Society and be judged as to my eligibility. My subsequent career has proved that I should not have been their worst choice; but after my address to them on Progress in Freethought, their Fundamentalists (for there is as high a percentage of such in the National Secular Society as in the Salvation Army) went white with rage, and made Standring aware that I had rather less chance of election than the Archbishop of Canterbury. My demonstration that the Trinity is not an arithmetical impossibility, but the commonplace union of father, son, and spirit in one person; that the doctrine of the Immaculate Conception is an instalment of the sacred truth that all conceptions are immaculate; that the Roman Catholic worship of the Madonna is in effect a needed addition of The Mother to The Father in The Godhead; and that any clever Jesuit could convert an average Secularist to Roman Catholicism, froze the marrow in their bones. Mrs Besant's conversion to Theosophy had not then shocked and shaken them.

Charles Watts, one of the ablest Secularist leaders, called himself neither Atheist nor Agnostic, but Rationalist. This was a stronger position, being a positive one, than the Atheism of Bradlaugh, though Bradlaugh's heroic personality kept him in the centre of the stage until his victory over the House of Commons extinguished and finally killed him. But a profession of Rationalism implies the belief that reason is not only method, but motive; and I was too critical a reasoner to make this mistake. I knew that Robespierre, when he set up a Goddess of Reason, soon found out that reason is only a machinery of thought, and had to agree with Voltaire that if there were no God it would be necessary to invent one. To govern men, practical rulers must reckon with honor, conscience, public spirit, social compunction, patriotism, self-sacrifice in pursuit of science and power over circumstances: in short, the apriorist virtues as well as their opposite vices: all inevitable but irrational. As I used to put it prosaically, reason can discover for you the best way—bus or tram, underground or taxi—to get from Piccadilly Circus to Putney, but cannot explain why you should want to go to Putney instead of staying in Piccadilly. Rationalism was also associated with Materialism; and I was and still am a Vitalist to whom vitality, though the hardest of hard facts, is a complete mystery. I have to deal constantly in reason and with matter; but I am neither a Rationalist nor a Materialist.

At least, it may be said, I might have called myself an Evolutionist. But at that time it was generally assumed that Darwin invented Evolution. He had done just the opposite. He had shewn that many of the evolutionary developments ascribed to a divine creator could have been produced accidentally without purpose or even consciousness. This process he called Natural Selection. The anti-clerical anti-Bible reaction was then so strong among the sceptical intelligentsia that they swallowed Natural Selection hook, line, and sinker. Weismann, then the most prominent neo-Darwinian, insisted that all our gestures and actions are mere reflexes.

This was all very well as far as it went; but the farseeing Samuel Butler, after being carried away by the reaction for six weeks, suddenly realized that by banishing purpose from natural history Darwin had, as Butler put it, banished mind from the universe. It soon began to appear that he had banished morality also; for Science, with a capital S, the new substitute for religion, claimed exemption from all decent and humane considerations. It idolized half-witted monomaniacs like Lister and Pavlov; established vivisection as the only avenue to biological science; flourished childish amateur statistics as recklessly as the Fundamentalists flourished what they called Christian evidence; declared that as there is no chemical difference between a live body and a dead one there is no scientific difference at all; rejected the harmless poetic rite of baptism as a barbarous superstition, and substituted fifty poisonous inoculations all warranted to make us immune from disease; prophesied the extinction of terrestrial life through the cooling of the sun; and generally plunged into an orgy of fanatical credulity and bigotry that at last provoked an outcry for a return to Christianity, or to any creed that has a place in it for Micah's postulate of justice, mercy, and humility before the enormity of our ignorance and the crudity of our mental processes. Darwinians who would have faced martyrdom sooner than deny their faith in Darwin or affirm a belief in God, were sometimes, when women or money were concerned, conscienceless rascals.

What then am I, an artist-biologist, to call myself when asked to define my religion? I am a Catholic because I am a Communist (the two words mean the same) intelligent enough to perceive that our civilization, such as it is, could not exist for a week without its vast Communist basis of policed roads and bridges, water supplies and street lamps, courts of justice, schools, churches, legislatures, administrations, common and statutory law, armies, navies, air forces, etc. all staring in the faces of the ignorant majority of people to whom Communist is only a term of vulgar abuse, and Communism an epitome of everything evil and infamous. But if I call myself a Catholic I am taken to be a member of one or other of the established Christian Churches, all self-styled Catholic, whether Roman, Anglican, Greek, or what not, and all saturated with opiate fancies such as the Atonement, dear to the dishonest who, dreading the bugbear of a brimstone hell, dare not sin for six days without being washed clean in the blood of the Lamb on the seventh, and all clinging to a fiction of personal immortality, which anesthetizes the fear of death for the average man. "The average man is a coward" said Mark Twain.

As to the cardinal Christian precept "Love one another" I, contemplating humanity in the persons of a few rich ladies and gentlemen confronted by a multitude of poor working folk, glorying in warfare, and wallowing in superstition, not only do not love them but dislike them so much that they must be replaced by more sensible animals if civilization is to be saved. I really cannot love Hitlers and Pavlovs and their idolaters any more than I could have loved the saintly Torquemada or the esthetic Nero.

If I call myself a Vitalist I shall be classed as a Materialist by the scientists who admit the existence of a life force but conceive it as purely mechanical like steam or electricity.

If I call myself simply an Evolutionist I shall be listed as a Darwinian. Yet if I repudiate Darwin it will be assumed that I attach no importance to the part played in human destiny by Natural Selection and by Reason; for the popular imagination works only in extremes: soot or whitewash, Right or Left, white or black. I am neither white nor black, but a classical grey, being very ignorant. All cats are grey in the dark.

I do not accept even the almost unquestioned sequence of Cause and Effect. It is the other way about with me. Bar pure accident, it is the aim, the purpose, the intended effect, that produces its so-called cause. If I shoot my neighbor it is not the fault of my gun and its trigger, nor is the rope the cause of my execution. Both are the effects of my intention to murder and the jury's sense of justice.

And so, as Bergson is the established philosopher of my sect, I set myself down as a Creative Evolutionist. And at that I should leave it, being too old a dog to pick up new tricks, were it not that I am still asked where God comes into my religion. When I parry such questions by "Where does He come into yours?" the two replies come to the same. The Churches have to postulate a God Almighty who, obviously, is either not almighty or not benevolent; for the world is crowded with evil as much as with good to such an extent that many of its ablest thinkers, from Ecclesiastes to Shakespear, have been pessimists; and the optimists have had to postulate a devil as well as a god. Both have had to reckon with the operation of a natural agency which the Churches call Providence and the scientists Phlogiston, Functional Adaptation, Natural Selection, Vis Naturae Medicatrix, the Necessary Myth, and Design in the Universe. I have called it the Life Force and the Evolutionary Appetite. Bergson called it the *Élan Vitale,* Kant the Categorical Imperative, Shakespear the "divinity that shapes our ends, rough-hew them how we will." They all come to the same thing: a mysterious drive towards greater power over our circumstances and deeper understanding of Nature, in pursuit of which men and women will risk death as explorers or martyrs, and sacrifice their personal comfort and safety against all prudence, all probability, all common sense.

As this unaccountable agency confronts every religion alike as a hard fact in spite of its many different names, it might as well be called Providence, which is the most expressive vernacular word for it. Thus much of the difference between the crudest Evangelism and Creative Evolution is found in administrative practice to be imaginary. Certainly the Bible Gods, of whom there are at least five, are all held on paper to be almighty, infallible, omnipotent and omniscient, whereas the Life Force, however benevolent, proceeds by trial and error and creates the problem of evil by its unsuccessful experiments and its mistakes. No practical administrative authority has ever been able to function on the assumption that almighty power, infallibility, and omniscience exist, or have ever existed or will exist in the world. When an atheist becomes a Plymouth Brother, or vice versa, the final comment is *plus ça change, plus c'est la même chose.* The infallibility of God is a fiction that may be as necessary politically as the infallibility of the Pope or of the Judicial Committee of the House of Lords; but it is a fiction all the same.

It matters hardly at all what our denominations are; and I must disclaim any design to impose my denomination on others. I do not forget the warning of Jesus that if we try to clear established religions of their weeds we may pull up the wheat as well and leave the husbandmen without any religion. I detest the doctrine of the Atonement, holding that ladies and gentlemen cannot as such possibly allow anyone else to expiate their sins by suffering a cruel death. But I know as a hard fact that Methodism, which is saturated with this abhorrent superstition, changed our colliers and their wives and mothers from savages into comparatively civilized beings; and that any attempt to convert them to Creative Evolution would have made them more dangerous savages than ever, with no scruples, no personal god (the only sort of God they could believe in), and no fear of hell to restrain them. To change a credulous peasantry to a sceptical one by inculcating a negative atheism plus a science beyond the reaches of their brains may make an end of civilization, not for the first time. It may even make an end of mankind, as it has already made an end of diplodoccus and dinosaur, mammoth and mastodon. Creative Evolution can replace us; but meanwhile we must work for our survival and development as if we were Creation's last word. Defeatism is the wretchedest of policies.

14

BIOGRAPHERS' BLUNDERS CORRECTED

The Right Honorable Winston Churchill, M.P., P.C.

"I was dragged to Low Church and Chapel."

Never. In Irish Protestant circles Church means Low Church (or perhaps Ritualist if there are candles on the altar); and Roman Catholic churches are called chapels. The distinction between Roman Catholic and Protestant overrides all the distinctions between Dissenters and Conformists clung to in England and Wales. In Ireland you are either a Protestant or you are not. If you are, it does not matter whether you go to the formerly Established Episcopal parish church, the Methodist meeting house, or the Presbyterian church: you may find the Squire or the Deputy Lieutenant among the Dissenters if he prefers their services. But should he put his foot inside the Roman Catholic chapel there would be the devil to pay.

The notion that I was brought up like a little Welsh Dissenter is wildly wrong. Our family atmosphere was one of derisive freethinking. By the time I was ten years old my parents had given up even the respectable pretence of church-going; and I myself, after reasoning the step quite deliberately, had stopped saying my prayers on the ground that I was an atheist. As my prayers were elaborate compositions of my own I felt that I was making a righteous sacrifice to principle in discarding them. It never occurred to my god-parents to concern themselves about the fact that Sonny Shaw was an Infidel.

"He speaks at hotels and at street corners."

Why hotels? I spoke everywhere else, from the British Association to the dock gates, the market places, and all the pitches in the country, but hardly ever in hotels. Henry James treated me with wondering awe because somebody told him that I had stopped one day on the Embankment and harangued the passers-by until I had quite a decent crowd. He asked me whether it was really true; and when I said it was, he exclaimed: "I could not do it. I could not bring myself to do it." I have always maintained that the open air is the best school for a public speaker.

My climax as a popular orator was at the General Election following the 1914-18 war, when to my astonishment the nearest streets were blocked with the crowds who could not get in.

My farewell to the platform and its vanities was at the

Metropolitan Opera House in New York in a quite successful ninety minutes' spellbinding; but I was tired for three days after it, and knew I was too old for the game.

Besides, the radio newsreel has shelved the platform. I can still do a few minutes' broadcasting effectively. Who would speak to hundreds of people when he can get at millions with half the effort?

"In 1889 he shows for the first time a little Marxian influence."

This is postdated. My last novel, An Unsocial Socialist, is pure Marx; and it was written in 1883. When the Fabian Society began in 1884, and I chose it for my platform, I had swallowed every word of Marx's that I could find in French. There was then practically nothing in English.

"Later on he threw Marx over for Mr Sidney Webb."

I never threw Marx over. In essentials I am as much a Marxist as ever. But when Philip Wicksteed, converted by Jevons, attacked the famous value theory of Marx, and I had to defend it because nobody better was available, I knew nothing of abstract economics.

For some years I hammered away at the subject, sitting under Wicksteed at a private society to which he lectured on the Jevonian theory. When I had thoroughly mastered what was left valid of Capitalist political economy I found that neither Marx nor anyone else in the Socialist movement understood it, and that as to abstract value theory Marx was

wrong and Wicksteed right. Of the law of rent, which is
fundamental in Socialism, Marx was simply ignorant, as his
footnote on Ricardo shews. His lack of administrative experience and of personal contacts with English society, both
proletarian and capitalistic, disabled him dangerously as a
practical politician in spite of his world-shaking exposure of
the villainies of Capitalism, and his grasp of its destiny in
the Communist Manifesto. In all this Sidney Webb, whose
prophet was John Stuart Mill, was not concerned. He had
followed Mill up to Mill's final Socialistic phase, and therefore needed no conversion by Marx. We both had the necessary *Weltverbesserungswahn*. Webb was all-of-one-piece, a
man of extraordinary ability and equally extraordinary sim-
plicity. Asquith described him as a saint. Without him I
might have been a mere literary wisecracker, like Carlyle and
Ruskin.

*"He has always preached the ownership of all forms of
wealth by the State; yet when the Lloyd George Budget imposed for the first time the slender beginnings of the super-
tax no one made a louder squawk than this already wealthy
Fabian."*

An ex-Chancellor of the Exchequer ought to know better.
Here are the facts. When the Suffragets were raging Mrs
Jacob Bright called on all propertied women to refuse to dis-
close their incomes to their husbands for declaration to the
Inland Revenue as part of his income. When filling my next

tax return I put down in the space provided for my wife's income that I did not know what it was, and had no legal power to compel her to disclose it. This staggered the Special Commissioners of Income Tax. At first they thought I was trying to evade the tax and make myself disagreeable. I pointed out that they could make a fancy assessment, and told them the figure at which I should demur, adding that as I had always insisted on my wife having a separate solicitor and banker (she having married a literary adventurer) I really did not know. I also explained about Mrs Jacob Bright, and what they had to expect if they did not find a way out. The result was the passing of a Bernard Shaw Relief Act which enabled husband and wife to make separate returns. When it became public vaguely that I had complained of something, it was concluded that it was the old grievance about being taxed at all.

Also I have steadily opposed all forms of taxation of capital, including estate duties (death duties), and insisted that only income is available for taxation. It is true that as if you have an income of five pounds a year your stockbroker can find somebody who will pay you from seventy to a hundred pounds ready money for it out of his spare cash, it is thoughtlessly assumed that a Chancellor of the Exchequer can always get as much money as he wants by multiplying the national income on paper by twenty, and assuming that the total can be collected at any moment by the tax collector. This is a ruinous fallacy. Capital and Credit are, for public purposes, fictitious categories. I wish I could make a much louder squawk about it; for some fool of a Labor Chancellor may easily be humbugged into taxing capital as such, and producing nothing but a Stock Exchange in which there are all sellers and no buyers, with capital values at zero and nothing doing.

"The Red Flag is dubbed by this most brilliant of Socialist intellectuals 'the burial march of a monkey.' "

Not quite accurate. I called it the funeral march of a fried eel.

The following refers to my visit to Russia in 1931.

"Multitudes of well-drilled demonstrators were served out with their red scarves and flags. The massed bands blared. Loud cheers from sturdy proletarians rent the welkin."

Pure imagination. Not a band, not a flag, not a red scarf, not a street cheer from one end of the trip to the other, though I was certainly treated as if I were Karl Marx in person, and given a grand reception (a queer mixture of public meeting, snack bar banquet, and concert) in the Hall of Nobles, which holds 4000 people and was crammed. The speeches were short. One of the concert performers wore evening dress, which seemed an absurd anachronism. One of the orators was in shirt and trousers, which seemed natural enough. Lunacharsky spoke. He and Litvinoff went about with me a good deal because, as I soon discovered, they wanted to see the wonders of Sovietism, which they had never had time to see before. Every possible civility and facility was heaped on me without any ceremony; and the absence of ceremony and platform bunk made it extraordinarily pleasant.

The climax of the tour was an interview with Stalin. The sentry at the Kremlin who asked who we were was the only soldier I saw in Russia. Stalin played his part to perfection, receiving us as old friends, and letting us talk ourselves dry before he modestly took the floor. Our party was Lord and Lady Astor, Phil Kerr (the late Marquess of Lothian), and myself. Litvinoff and a few other Russians were present. On our way in we passed through three or four offices. In each of them sat an official at a writing table. We guessed a revolver handy in the drawer.

The proceedings opened with a violent attack by Lady Astor, who told Stalin that the Bolshevists did not know how to treat children. Stalin, for a moment taken aback, said contemptuously with a gesture "In England you B E A T children."

Lady Astor promptly told him (in effect) not to be a damned fool, and to send some sensible woman to London to be instructed at Margaret Macmillan's camp in Deptford in how children of five should be handled and dressed and taught. Stalin immediately made a note of her address. We thought this mere politeness. But hardly had we got home when the sensible woman arrived with half a dozen others hungry for instruction. They were duly taken to Deptford, on which much Astor money has been lavished.

Then we came to politics; and Phil took the floor as a man who had read Karl Marx and knew all about scientific Communism. He explained that the English Liberal Party had split, many of them to the Right, leaving the rest sheep without a shepherd, unable to join the Labor Party because the Labor Party was politically infantile. What was needed was a move to the Left of the Labor Party by a party of Scientific Communism under the leadership of Lloyd George. Phil suggested that Stalin should invite Ll. G. officially to Moscow, and shew him all the wonders of Soviet Russia.

Nothing could exceed the good humor with which Stalin received this proposal. He was evidently amused by it, as I was. His reply, lengthy and pleasantly courteous, but apparently full of fun, was translated for us to the effect that an official invitation to the accomplice of Wrangel in the White Army invasion was not possible, but that if Ll. G. would come along in his private capacity he would receive every attention and facility.

Lord Astor strove to impress on Stalin that there was plenty of good feeling towards the Soviet in England, and nothing to prevent the friendliest understanding in the future. In fact he went so far that I had to warn Stalin that Lloyd George, implacably hostile to Bolshevism, was not wholly unrepresentative in that respect. I asked Stalin whether he had ever heard of Oliver Cromwell and his precept, preserved in the refrain of a song well known in Ireland,

Put your trust in God, my boys,
And keep your powder dry.

When he had taken this in he intimated that he would
certainly keep his powder dry. He left God out of the question. I then asked what about inviting Mr Churchill to
Russia. His geniality became, I thought, slightly sardonic as
he replied that he would be delighted to see Mr Churchill
in Moscow.

His sense of humor was throughout very evident. He can
laugh.

When we left (after midnight) we thought we had been
a little over half an hour in the presence. Our watches scored
two hours and thirtyfive minutes.

Sidmouth,
September 1937

The Late Professor O'Bolger

Professor O'Bolger was the son of an Irish Police Inspector.
He was an admirer of my work to the extent of devoting
such time as he could spare from his professorial work to a
biography of me; and I wrote him many letters in answer to
his appeals for information. But when the biography was
written and offered to an American publisher, it contained
statements so defamatory that the publisher, though accept-
ing it on its literary merits, demanded a certificate of my con-

firmation and approval. How impossible it was for me to give such a certificate will be made clear by what follows. Accordingly, the book was not published; but as the manuscript is in the hands of the author's executors, and may after my death come to light under the title of The Truth About Bernard Shaw, or the like, I had better make public my reply to it.

Though Professor O'Bolger adopted literature as his profession he inherited his father's police attitude and technique, always testing the statements and the evidence of accused or suspected persons with a view to their prosecution for breaches of the law, and collecting evidence as to their personal characters. In this there was no question of esthetic criticism: the sole issue was whether the facts would bear a construction of illegality or infamy. In short, the professor went to work neither as critic nor biographer, but simply as a detective, without the responsibility of an official inspector or an Attorney General.

Here is as much of my comment as I need record here.

Parknasilla, Kenmare,
Co. Kerry.
7th August 1919

DEAR O'BOLGER,

You will certainly be the death of me. As you describe it, my story is one in which the kindly hero, my father, was driven to drink by his wife's infidelity, and finally abandoned to die in the workhouse.

Must I tell you the facts over again? And if I do will they be any more effectual in driving this fictitious item of police news out of your distracted head than my own authentic account?

Just put my mother's singing master and colleague, G. J. Lee, out of your head for a moment. He has not yet appeared on the scene. My father is a middle-aged bachelor, "nobody's enemy but his own." Nobody hates him because nobody fears him.

He is something of a humorist, and writes verses occasionally to amuse people. Sir Robert Shaw, Bart., of Bushey Park, Terenure, is his second cousin; and he ranks himself a man of feudal family, but has no property, being a younger son downstart. A fair proportion of his numerous brothers and sisters are in prosperous circumstances and unchallengeable social positions. He drinks. It is not a convivial weakness: it is a neurosis, pathological, miserable; and its victims are earnest teetotallers protesting and preaching against their curse. It has appeared in the family before, and is destined to appear again among my cousins and their children. Nobody mentions it to strictly brought up young ladies, held immune from unpleasant subjects until they are married.

My mother is a strictly brought up young lady. So strictly brought up, in fact, by the aunt whose heiress apparent she is, that she knows nothing about marriage nor housekeeping nor anything unladylike. For some time she is welcomed by the prosperous Shaws: Sir Robert likes her; and the others regard her as a social asset. But my father gets drunk at their dinners and parties; and it is impossible to invite him again, or his wife without him. Impecuniosity, ostracism, three children, a house rented at £30 a year or thereabouts, a drunken husband obviously incapable of much success as a merchant: this was the lot of my mother when Lee, roaming in search of singers, players, and material of all sorts for his musical activities, discovered her voice and trained it. I have told you all this in much greater detail; and your conclusion is that my mother committed adultery with a musical impostor, and drove her kindly, sober, heroic husband to drink.

My father did not die in the workhouse. In his last years he was left alone in Dublin by his wife and children for the very solid reason that he could not support them, and that life with him had absolutely no prospects for them. In doing so, they took off his shoulders a burden he was unable to bear and glad to discard, though he had given up drinking, and was now the most inoffensive of mortals. What he could do for them he did, which was to send them a pound a week until he died. Meanwhile he lived very comfortably in lodgings in the Appian Way (a highly respectable suburban residential quarter), much appreciated by his landlady, and in due time was gathered to his fathers in Mount Jerome Cemetery in the fullest Shavian gentility. I believe it was the happiest time of his life. No more Lee, no more wife, no more grown-up children. Towards the end, one or two newspaper cuttings and reviews convinced him that his son was going to achieve his father's somehow missed destiny and be "a great man."

Subject to these unheroic facts you may write as kindly of my father as you like. He was really, as men go, humane and likeable. He once told me how in his boyhood he had found a stray cat, and brought it home with him and fed it. But next morning he let his dog course it and kill it. He was still conscience stricken by this atrocity, and warned me that no man capable of it deserved or could have any good fortune or happiness afterwards. He was full of self-reproaches and humiliations when he was not full of secret jokes, and was either biting his moustache and whispering deepdrawn damns, or shaking with silent paroxysms of laughter. His partner in business was comparatively rough mannered; and my father believed that the little tacts and kindlinesses and genialities with which he allayed the susceptibilities hurt by his partner kept the business alive. They certainly helped.

But there is nothing in your heredity point, because, as it happens, my mother was also very kind, incapable of striking a child or an animal, hating to see a flower thrown away or picked to pieces. Many women with her provocation would have hated my father: she was not in the least bitter about him. She had no respect for him in the common sense of the word, as he could do nothing dramatically interesting or effective; but she took him as he was, in the kindly Irish fashion, without trumping up a moral case against him or blaming him. We were all like that, more or less: his position in the household was just what he was capable of taking: he was Papa in the fullest sense always; and the dynamic Lee got none of the affection Papa inspired.

Lee's failure in London, disguised as it was by a few years of fashionable success, was due wholly to the social conditions which compelled him to be a humbug or to starve. My mother, who followed him to London to take up music as a profession and launch my sister Lucy as a *prima donna,* was as available as in Dublin. But the moment she found he had abandoned "The Method" in his teaching, and was pretending to enable his pupils to sing like Patti in 12 lessons, she gave him up, and had not seen him for years when he died: an event which did not disturb her one jot. No more, for that matter, did my father's. The death of my sister Agnes was her only grief in that kind. My father, by the way, found something in a funeral which tickled his sense of humor; and this characteristic I have inherited. I never grieve; but I do not forget.

So much for your estimate of my mother's wifely virtues! Your remarks on my economics are not criticism. You keep conscientiously contradicting things I never said, and complaining of propositions which, if I had ever advocated them, would have consigned me to a mental hospital. My plays are no more economic treatises than Shakespear's.

It is true that neither Widowers' Houses nor Major Barbara could have been written by an economic ignoramus, and that

Mrs Warren's Profession is an economic exposure of the White Slave traffic as well as a melodrama. There is an economic link between Cashel Byron, Sartorius, Mrs Warren, and Undershaft: all of them prospering in questionable activities. But would anyone but a buffleheaded idiot of a university professor, half crazy with correcting examination papers, infer that all my plays were written as economic essays, and not as plays of life, character, and human destiny like those of Shakespear or Euripides?

My views on education are not novel nor eccentric in any way. But I have pointed out that schools and schoolmasters, as we have them today, are not popular as places of education and teachers, but rather prisons and turnkeys in which children are kept to prevent them disturbing and chaperoning their parents. Also that civics and religion should be classed as necessary technical education for civilized life, not optional liberal education for culture. I would make them both compulsory and controversial. Liberal education should be voluntary and should be conducted in voluntary organizations. These are propositions to be discussed. The one concerning the school and the schoolmaster has no more to do with education than burglary with banking, and no less. If you mix up the two you will get hopelessly muddled and nag yourself into lunacy.

You are all wrong with your university twaddle about the ambitious clever boy. I never was ambitious: like Hamlet I lack ambition. I am not, and never have been, phenomenally clever. I have "risen" by sheer gravitation and the accident of possessing a lucrative talent. My timid want of push kept me a penniless burden on my harassed parents until I was nearly thirty. Your romance of a clever and ambitious youth, full of Carlyle and Emerson (I had never read a word of either) writhing under the ignominy of being an office clerk, is miles off the target. Office clerks are the proudest beings on earth. They despise professors as helplessly unpractical schoolboys who have never escaped into adult responsibility and knowledge of business. It is true that I was uncomfortable in an office because I was a round peg in a square hole; but it never occurred to me to be ashamed of it.

If it does not suit your story to believe that Lee was in his way a genius, better alter your story. I tell you that he was; and I know better than you, being an expert musical critic who has heard all the great conductors of my time and heard the pupils of all the great teachers of singing. You say you have no evidence. Have you looked? A German would probably fill several pages with a list of the concerts and festivals conducted by Lee in Dublin, and the works performed at them. He would dig them out of the newspaper files. You can do it if you want to waste your time and be unreadable. What other traces can a conductor leave?

When you say that poverty consists not in want but in mismanaged distribution, you mean that poverty exists not because there is not wealth enough to go round, but because it is not sent round fairly. You are wrong. There is not wealth enough to go round. But with Socialism there might be.

And now accept my hearty curse for putting me to the intolerable task of telling you over again what I have already told you very fully and carefully.

Go away and recuperate. Your brains are addled by your unnatural employment. I warn you that it is as easy to ruin a man by giving him more literary material than he can digest, as by giving him more capital than he can manage. Your digestion just now is very much out of order.

My Late Australian Cousin Charles Shaw

DEAR COUSIN CHARLES,

In Australia society is much more promiscuous than it was in Ireland in the nineteenth century. The Shaws were snobs necessarily, like all Irish Protestants; but you have to bear in mind the different sorts of snobbery. When my father told me I must not play with a schoolfellow whose father kept shop as an ironmonger he was telling me what all fathers in his position had to tell their sons to prevent their making what he believed to be undesirable acquaintances. When I was told that all Roman Catholics went to hell it was impossible for me not to infer that they were an inferior species with whom a Protestant Shaw could not fitly associate. There were two social frontiers strictly drawn: the first between wholesaler and retailer, and the other between the Church of Rome and the Episcopal Church of Ireland, which was then the established Church. No Shaw could form a social acquaintance with a shopkeeper nor with a Roman Catholic; and naturally the Shaw parents impressed that fact on their children and thereby made arrant snobs of them.

But there is another department of snobbery which is less compulsory; and your book is amusingly full of it. This is the snobbery of the clan: the conviction that "the Shaws" were a superior family with dominant noses, descended from or belonging to the landed gentry. To an Irish Shaw this seemed a fact of natural history.

We still jib at a description of us as middle class, as did the Shaw who became police chief in Hobart. That is the sort of snobbery my emigrant eldest uncle took to Australia. All you can do with it is to make goodnatured fun of it. In a post-Marxian age it will not wash.

Your attempt to prove that my father did not wreck his marriage by drinking is the most desperate enterprise in the book; and it has led you to libel him atrociously by comparing him to the father of Erewhon Butler. Butler feared and hated his father intensely, with good reason, as his father's notion of bringing him up in a godly way was simply to beat humanity out of him and Latin grammar into him. Now nobody could hate my father. When I recall certain occasions on which I was inconsiderate to him I understand how Dr Johnson stood in the rain in Lichfield to expiate the same remorse. My father was unlucky and untrained and unsuccessful; but he conquered his miserable drink neurosis (for it did make him miserable) when one Sunday he fell down on our doorstep in a fit which gave him a thorough fright, and made him understand that he was destroying himself. From that time he drank no more.

When nevertheless we all deserted him, he must have found himself much happier; and I am much indebted to you for giving me the evidence of this: to wit, that he was able to renew his relations with his brothers and sisters. Two things had detached him from them. First, the drink neurosis. At one of the family parties at Bushy Park, he got so drunk that he was written off as socially impossible. We were no longer visited by nor invited by his brothers and sisters; and I no longer saw anything of my cousins.

This was hard enough on him; but what was harder was that he could not find society in his own house. When we made a joint household with George John Vandalear Lee, my mother's musical colleague, his mesmeric energy and enterprise reduced my father to nullity in the house.

When his children had grown too big for him to play with, and their suspense as to whether he would come home drunk or sober never ceased, he got practically no comfortable society from them. His relatives did not want to see him; and my mother did not want to see his relatives: she was interested only in people who could sing; and they were mostly Catholics, better citizens and much pleasanter friends, but not proper company for a Protestant Shaw.

I leave you to imagine the effect you produce on me when you take your stand firmly on the ground that no Shaw could possibly be anything so vulgar as a drunkard, and that therefore I must be a jocose liar. If you had been through that time with me you would not see anything in it to joke about. But do not rush to the other extreme and conclude that all the Shaws were inebriates. Only three out of eleven drank; and two of them, my father and William (Barney), suddenly gave it up long after their cases seemed hopeless.

Now consider the sequel when I, at 20 years of age, the last member of the family to live with my father, deserted him like the others and fled to London. It really was the consummation of a blessed relief for him. His wife had already gone. When his son, who, in the religious revival produced by the visit of the famous Evangelists Moody and Sankey to Dublin, had written a letter to Public Opinion practically declaring himself an atheist, went too, what was there to prevent his return to his clan? You tell me they took him back and made him as happy as we had made him wretched. I am delighted to hear it.

Those lunches you describe with his brother Henry on Sundays were impossible whilst we were with him. He was received by his sister Emily Carroll as a wit of the first order. When I found the only survivor of Aunt Emily's brood at Eastbourne the other day, she told me some of the funny things he used to say. I cannot believe that he ever wanted to see us again; but there was not the slightest ill feeling between us; and when it happened that my sister Lucy was in Dublin when he died, which he did instantaneously in the happiest manner, they were on affectionate terms.

Our indifference to oneanother's deaths marked us as a re-markably unsentimental family. And your determination to find us full of Victorian sentiment, including romantic beauty for all the women and dauntless courage for all the men, has culminated in your fancy sketch of my sister Lucy's life and character which is not only untrue, but the very opposite to the truth. Lucy, away from home, was everybody's darling: she broke many hearts, but never her own. When she was middle-aged, she married: why, I cannot tell you. My best guess is that she liked her husband's family, who were pillars of the Irvingite Church and highly respectable solid people. Her mother-in-law had discovered that the pleasantest place to live is in bed, where she remained for 15 years or so until she died. Lucy had always fought shy of the opportunities her good looks and her singing gave her of getting into feudal society: she knew that she had neither the money nor, as a professional singer, the social standing to be comfortable there, so she very wisely kept among people who looked up to her and petted her rather than those who looked down their noses at her. She had no use for the Shaw pretensions, nor for the country-gentility of her maternal stock. Yet she hated Bohemianism and was ashamed of it. Her bedridden mother-in-law saw what was the matter, and set herself to give Lucy the social training she bitterly needed; for my mother, herself tyrannically over-trained, left us all to train ourselves; and Lucy, who had always resented this, was greatly relieved when her new mother won her eternal gratitude by teaching her how to behave herself.

Her husband was a little dumpling of an ex-insurance clerk whose pretty face seemed to be carved on a bladder of lard. His one ambition was to be a leading tenor in light opera. His clerkship in the colonies enabled him to save £50; and with this sum he bribed the manager of a touring light opera company to allow him to sing the principal tenor part for one night. After this, I suppose, they could not very well turn him into the street. He sang with difficulty; but still he could sing a bit; and his tastes made him quite at home in the theatre. He was addicted to gambling and to women. In the theatre he met Lucy and married her. She soon got tired of him and banished him, resuming her way of living as a free spinster. This had gone on for some years when she learnt accidentally that at the time of her marriage he had been attached to another woman. In a burst of fury she came to me and said she must have a divorce. As she had already practically divorced him I suggested that the operation was superfluous; but she was determined to be legally rid of him; and he was quite willing to leave her petition undefended if all claims for alimony or damages were waived. Accordingly, the divorce went through; and Lucy resumed her spinster name.

Then came the Shavian touch. Later on he turned up again, lonely and at a loss for somewhere to spend his evenings. Lucy immediately tolerated him as a waif and stray, though as a husband she had found him unbearable. So he became her frequent visitor until he died, when his place was taken by his very capable brother, who was manager of one of London's monster multiple shops. Lucy survived them all without shedding a tear. Our parents had been dead a long time. I was the only immediate relative left; and I visited her only at very long intervals when we had some business to discuss. One afternoon, when her health was giving some special anxiety, I called at her house and found her in bed. When I had sat with her a little while she said: "I am dying." I took her hand to encourage her and said, rather conventionally, "Oh no: you will be all right presently." We were silent then; and there was no sound except from somebody playing the piano in the nearest house (it was a fine evening and all the windows were open) until there was a very faint flutter in her throat. She was still holding my hand. Then her thumb straightened. She was dead.

The doctor came in presently; and, as I had to register the death, I asked him what cause of death he would put in the certificate, adding that I supposed it was tuberculosis, from which she had suffered for many years following an attack of pneumonia which had ended her stage career. He said no: her tuberculosis had been completely cured. I said "What then?" He replied: "Starvation." I remonstrated, assuring him that I had provided for her better than that. He then told me that since the 1914-18 war he had never been able to make her eat enough. During the air raids an anti-aircraft gun, planted just outside her garden, had broken all the windows and crockery in her house, and shellshocked her badly. They had taken her away to Devon, out of range of the German bombers; but she never recovered her appetite.

Not knowing her circle of friends I did not invite anyone to her cremation at Golders Green; but when I got there I found the chapel crowded with her adorers. In her will she had expressly forbidden any religious service; but with all those people there I felt that I could not have her thrown on the fire like a scuttle of coals; so I delivered a funeral oration, and finished by reciting the dirge from Cymbeline because

> Fear no more the lightning-flash,
> Nor the all-dreaded thunder-stone

so nearly fitted what the doctor told me.

Lucy had literary faculty enough to have one or two stories, written in the style of Rhoda Broughton, accepted by the old Family Herald. In middle life she perpetrated a book of which one of her admirers, who happened to be a publisher, brought out an edition. It is supposed to be a series of letters addressed by an old woman to a young one, advising her as to her conduct in life. It was so cynical that it revolted my mother, and almost shocked even me.

The rest you must discover from my notes on your type-script. They will give you some eye-openers as to the family which you have been able to idolize to your heart's content in Australia.

BIOGRAPHERS' BLUNDERS CORRECTED

To Henry Charles Duffin

I have read the proof sheets of your Quintessence of Bernard Shaw (why not of Shavianism?) with much less anguish than books about myself usually cause me. I will come at once to the points which seem to me open to criticism; and I will have to take them in the order in which they occur in the book without any attempt at continuity.

Page 9. You imply here that I have declared my plays to be better than Shakespear's. This is not so. In the preface to Plays for Puritans, there is a chapter headed "Better than Shakespear?" (note the ?) in which I deal with the question raised by the fact that two of my leading historical characters had been dramatized by Shakespear. My reply contains no hint of your version of it, which is, I think, a reminiscence of my preface to The Irrational Knot. What I said was, to put it shortly, that no one can write a better play than Lear, nor a better opera than Don Giovanni: in short, that the summits of possible achievement, as far as artistic execution is concerned, have been already attained in all the arts. But this does not mean that Shakespear's Caesar cannot be surpassed as history by any quite ordinary playwright who has read Mommsen and Ferrero as well as Plutarch, nor that Ibsen, on his own ground, does not leave Shakespear nowhere in subtlety, intensity, and penetration. It was the overwhelming contrast with Ibsen that explains my Saturday Review campaign against the spurious part of Shakespear's reputation.

153

But the notion that I ever claimed crudely that my plays, or anybody's plays, were better written than Shakespear's, is absurd.

Page 15. All that stuff about smoking is silly, and means simply that you are a smoker. Have you ever taken a country walk to a railway station, and then stepped into a smoking carriage? If you can do so without at least a momentary disgust, you must be lost to all sense of smell. When I returned from the Carpentier-Beckett fight, I had to change every stitch of clothing before I could approach anyone without an apology. What is the use of ignoring such experiences, and writing of "the inoffensive lover of the peaceful pipe"? I am, of course, in practice tolerant of smoking, because otherwise I should cut myself off from human society. But I do not shut my eyes (or nose) to the fact that it is a noisome and loathsome habit. Your statement that I "modify my objections to smoking when, as in the case of a woman, it is a symbol of revolt" is pure fancy. I hate to see a woman smoking; but I do not on that account represent women in my plays as non-smokers. Vivie Warren smokes cigars because her living original did so. Louka smokes cigarettes because Bulgarian girls do. They do it just as Broadbent in John Bull's Other Island does. But I should not do even that if it were not possible for an actor or actress to pretend to smoke without really doing it, as Winston Churchill is said to do. You say that "the tobacco question is a purely individual one." Then why have places to be set apart for smoking, and the practice forbidden elsewhere, if nobody is affected but the smoker? Take my advice: give it up. Try knitting instead. My gardener, a non-smoker, knits.

Page 16 (and much elsewhere). You say I "blame" Shakespear and Dickens for making drunkenness and shrewishness a matter for laughter. I do not blame them: I say, like Keegan, that "every jest is an earnest in the womb of time." Many of my own most serious propositions have occurred to me first as jokes. You see this evolution in Dickens himself. Mrs MacStinger in Dombey & Son is a joke. As Mrs Gargery in Great Expectations she is no joke. As to Shakespear on drunkenness, compare Sir Toby Belch with Cassio and the king in Hamlet. Erewhon and The Authoress of The Odyssey must first have struck Butler as whimsicalities. Many things of which I have made fun in my plays will be made tragedy by future playwrights.

Page 34. "Butler is one of the most lovable men who ever lifted pen." You wrote this before the appearance of Festing Jones's Memoir. If you have by chance read my review of the Memoir in The Manchester Guardian you will understand why I do now tell you that the word lovable is rather a daring one unless you hold that all men of genius are lovable. Butler was much more like his father than he suspected. The Reverend Theobald Butler with a strong mind instead of a weak one would have been very like his great son.

Page 43. Do you seriously think that William Blake should have written The Marriage of Heaven and Hell in terms of

Parish Magazine morality? Just try the experiment of rewriting The Devil's Disciple in those terms, and see what sort of play you will get out of it. I have never met anyone who was in the least puzzled by Dick Dudgeon. Have you? It is one of your good points that where you are clever you are obviously very clever, and where you are stupid you are obviously very stupid.

Page 53. Dogmatic toleration is nonsense: I would no more tolerate the teaching of Calvinism to children if I had power to persecute it than the British Raj tolerated suttee in India. Every civilized authority must draw a line between the tolerable and the intolerable.

Page 72. Have I really conveyed to you that when it comes to the relations of the sexes there is no female but the spider female? Ann Whitefield in Man and Superman does not fill up my field of vision as completely as she has filled up yours. The tragedy of Mrs Knox in Fanny's First Play, mistaking Knox's transfiguration by carnal love for what Mrs George adored in the bishop from whom she kept so carefully apart, is not a spider tragedy; and Major Barbara, Lesbia Grantham, Lina Szczepanowska you have noted in subsequent passages as getting quite as far from the bee and the spider as my least philoprogenitive men. It seems to me that what is in your mind is the vast mass of people who are as nearly neuter in sex as it is possible for human beings to be. Ann is of course not typical of them. Then there are the people, also very numerous, who reason no more about sexual physiology and

156

psychology than about any other physiology and psychology. A spider probably thinks it spins its web and catches its prey for sport, or perhaps as a rite enjoined by some arachnean god, and does not know that it will die if it does not eat. But my sort of play would be impossible unless I endowed my characters with powers of self-consciousness and self-expression which they would not possess in real life. You could not have Esop's fables unless the animals talked.

However, there may be a genuine difference between us here. I am not sure that I shall not deal dramatically with the anti-maternal woman some day. I am by no means unacquainted with the species. I never met what you call (p. 82) "the broody hen type of woman who regards herself as, first and foremost, a child incubator"; but on the other hand I never met a woman—and I have put the question to some intensely anti-maternal ones—who, having borne a child, regretted that experience. On p. 84 you say, in this connection, "Of course, Shaw would call that cunning hypocrisy." I should not dream of saying anything so silly and ignorant.

Page 89. In speaking of jealousy you have committed a curious oversight which makes me doubt whether you have had much personal experience of jealousy. Julia in The Philanderer is as much a study of jealousy as Leontes in The Winter's Tale; yet you do not seem to have noticed that she is jealous. It is jealousy that makes her impossible. And on this point I may add that you do not seem to make any allowance for the considerable part of a playwright's *dramatis personae* which consists in studies from the living model. Some of my characters are close portraits: for others I have used a model just as a painter does. You write throughout as if all my characters were allegorical personifications, not persons.

Page 93. Here you suddenly assume that I, like ante-Marx Macaulay, see in history an advance in general enlightenment. I dont. Read the notes to Cæsar and Cleopatra, or the Revolutionist's Handbook; and you will see that I regard the Macaulayan delusion as a most dangerous one.

Page 96. "Crampton is a thoroughly likeable old fellow." A man who can like Crampton could like anybody.

Page 102. You forget that Gregory Lunn is actually in Mrs Juno's arms when his wife arrives with Juno. When he says that men have to make love to most women because it is impossible to talk to them, he is telling truth; but this does not save him when the woman is good company as well as seductive. The subject of the play is the overruling by the Life Force of bourgeois morality and the conscience founded on it. It is described by Byron's Don Juan in a passage you quote. Here it is shewn for the first time in action on the stage. Yet you see nothing in it, apparently, but a trivial remark by Gregory.

Pages 104-6. I do not want to abolish the family. The group of father, mother, and children, though by itself narrowing and unsocial, is the natural social unit.

Page 106. "The secret in the poet's heart" is the one you

describe as the most probable: that is, that the domestic life is not a poet's destiny: "life is nobler than that." The starry night, and not the cosy room with the paraffin lamp, is the place for him. Your alternative solution that "sooner or later she will come to me after all" is wildly silly.

Page 143. When Mrs Warren says that "the only way for a woman to provide for herself decently is for her to be good to some man that can afford to be good to her" she includes marriage, as you say; but she also points out that women with lucrative talents are independent of both marriage and prostitution as means of obtaining something better than a starvation wage. But this is only because exceptional talents have a scarcity value. You make the amazing comment that "if a woman cares, as most men do, to use higher talents and secure additional qualifications, she will be tolerably sure of doing well." The implication that a girl born in a fried fish shop in the east end can, if she likes, practise in all the liberal professions, shews that you have no vision of the real condition of the poor. "If they have no bread, why dont they eat cake?" is practical in comparison. Yet you point out that men, who have not the alternative of prostitution, are condemned to the same penury.

Page 146. Here you shew, not for the only time in the book, that you think of me only as a playwright. Yet for every play I have written I have made hundreds of speeches and published big books on Fabian Socialism. There is behind my plays a thought-out sociology which makes them fundamentally unlike those by authors to whom knowledge of society means that peas should not be eaten with a knife, nor a knight's wife called Lady Polly Jones instead of Lady Jones.

Your last section on pp. 146-7 is wrong all through. I never "realized the futility of preaching to empty pews." The pews were never empty: what I did realize was the futility of preaching to full ones. Crowded meetings butter no parsnips. You evidently have not followed my work as a Socialist; and you had better keep clear of it unless you are prepared to make a study of it, which will take you a long time.

As to the problem of evil I am not, as you say, "wisely content to leave it at its irony": on the contrary Blanco Posnet voices the question "What about the croup?", and answers it. There is a studied theory of Creative Evolution behind all my work; and its first complete statement is the third act of Man and Superman. It is the faith of Butler and Bergson. Your "inscrutable irony of God" is only stale Byronism and XIX century Agnosticism.

Page 158. The sense of honor cannot be "implanted in the child from without by its instructors": it is a divine spark in the child. Instructors can pervert it by making false applications of it (the public school code of honor, for example); but natural sense is always more or less in revolt against its perversions; and geniuses are always unmasking the impostures.

Page 161. You speak of my demand "that creeds shall be

MY FATHER IN HIS LAST YEARS

MY SISTER LUCINDA FRANCES

made credible." But you go on to assume that I demand that they should be made true and rational, which is another pair of shoes, carrying you to imagine that to me all men and women are rational, though you accept my comedies as demonstrations that they are not. Truth is often much less credible than legend.

What you are thinking of is my insistence on the demoralizing effect of creeds that ableminded persons cannot believe, with the result that they either turn their backs on religion and public life or else become hypocrites. The validity of the creed has nothing to do with this aspect of the matter. The point is that an established creed does a mischief when it is incredible that it does not do when it is credible, even though the incredible creed may be true and the credible false.

Page 186. There is a good deal of truth in your description of democracy as "stupidity armed with a gun"; but you miss the fact that in my sense "the lawyer, the priest, the literary man, and the politician" are on the whole more dangerous than the common folk who have not been stultified by the process which we call secondary education.

I have scribbled some marginal notes on the pages following 200, where I think you are occasionally merely petulant, as in your earlier references to smoking. You have probably not read my preface to The Educational Year Book for 1919, in which I have-out my quarrel with the schoolmaster, and state certain distinctions between technical and liberal education which I regard as important, especially that in which I class religious education as technical. As to the question of childbeating, I am, as far as I know, the only humanitarian writer who has said flatly that a child should not be protected from learning by experience that if it makes an unbearable nuisance of itself it will get its head clouted by some infuriated victim. But I have insisted that if teaching is to mean nothing but beating a child if it does not give set answers to set questions, then Squeers and Creakle are fully qualified schoolmasters, and the profession of teaching is not only an unskilled but an infamous one. Your own comments make me suspect you of having been a schoolmaster without any turn for teaching. You say I was an unschoolable boy at a bad school. But what is an unschoolable boy? I was greedy for knowledge, and interested in everything; but I could not read schoolbooks, though I could read almost anything else. The school, now known as Wesley College, was no doubt a bad one; but it was and is still among the best schools in the country. Shelley at Eton was an unschoolable boy at a bad school, but not in the sense you imply. I was probably the most teachable boy in Ireland; and if school taught me nothing except that a school is a prison and not a place of teaching, the conclusion is that pedagogy is not yet a science.

Pages 208-9. The character of Dubedat illustrates one of my pet theses, which is that no man is scrupulous all round. He has, according to his faculties and interests, certain points of honor, whilst in matters that do not interest him he is

careless and unscrupulous. One of the several models who
sat unconsciously for Dubedat was morbidly scrupulous as
to his religious and political convictions, and would have
gone to the gallows sooner than recant a syllable of them.
But he had absolutely no conscience about money and women:
he was a shameless seducer and borrower, not to say a thief.
In contrast with men who were scrupulously correct in their
family and business life he seemed a blackguard, and was a
blackguard; but there were occasions on which they cut a
very poor figure beside him: occasions when loyalty to their
convictions called for some risk and sacrifice. When Dubedat
says on his deathbed that he has fought the good fight, he
is quite serious. He means that he has not painted little girls
playing with fox terriers to be exhibited and sold at the Royal
Academy, instead of doing the best he could in his art. Much
as I have written against anarchic Bohemianism as the curse
of artists, and declared that there is no lack of clever people
but a great lack of sober honest and industrious ones, always
declining to offer a high order of talent as an excuse for a
low order of conduct, none the less I am aware that bourgeois
morality is largely a system of making cheap virtues a cloak
for expensive vices. Therefore I cannot endorse your dismissal
of Dubedat as a mere cad. He had his faith, and upheld it.

Pages 211-12. I have no special sympathy with "the criminal in his cell": I am revolted by the cruelty of putting anyone in a cell. My alternative, which is to kill the criminal

if he cannot be trusted at large, would not strike him as sympathetic. And I have no hatred of "physical violence of any sort." The late Cecil Chesterton elicited from me a very full explanation of my view. Physical violence is the weapon by which stupidity and villainy can always defeat and destroy mind and virtue. That this should need repetition today is only a proof of the thoughtless sentimentality that governs us. One of the first points of honor in civilized society should be that mental combats must not be fought out with fists nor crime by torture. Paul Jones's instinct was sound when he was prepared to kill a mutineer if necessary, but not to flog him.

But I must not plague you with any more cavils. I quite agree with your conclusion that the "brilliant" Shaw is only a preacher with four or five texts which would be dull enough if he were not a bit of an artist. You have caught the spirit of the plays and the gist of them in a way which would have been impossible if you had not enjoyed them; and you have enjoyed them to an extent which would have been impossible if the Life Force in you had not been keeping fairly in step with the Life Force in me. I did not expect you to do all my work over again by arguing every point down to the bedrock. But you have given people a very effective and competent recommendation to come to me and hear what I have to say to them; and for that I am much obliged, and have for once, read a book about myself conscientiously through

The Macmanus Biography in Winsten's G.B.S. 90

Page 33. As a picture of my state of mind when I crossed the Irish Channel nothing could be falser than this page. As far as I had any resolutions or intentions at all I left Ireland because I had no apparent future there; for in the interval between Lee's emigration and the literary and dramatic revival led by W. B. Yeats and Lady Gregory Dublin was an art Sahara. As to conquering London I no more dreamt of such a possibility than the poorest Irish peasant-emigrant dreamt of conquering the United States.

Page 33. My auburn hair was never really Highland red like my sister Agnes's. But I was a "blonde beast" of Danish type unmistakably.

Page 36. We always spoke of our grandmother's picturesque bungalow as Roundtown. I am told that it is now transmographied: half shops, half dwelling.

We Shaws were certainly not taught to "revere" the English connection. We regarded ourselves as a very distinguished section of it.

I never saw my father with a book in his hand. But he must have done some reading in his youth; for he knew Scott's novels, and encouraged me to read. I read The Pilgrim's Progress to him, and remember his telling me not to pronounce grievous as grevious.

Sir William Wilde overdid the operation on my father's eye. He cured the natural squint, but produced a worse one in the opposite direction.

My father's sense of humor was not "heavily exaggerated"; but he had a comedic love of anti-climax which I inherited. When the firm of Clibborn and Shaw was almost ruined by the bankruptcy of one of its debtors, Clibborn could not restrain his tears; but my father retreated to the warehouse and indulged in a laugh all to himself. Irishmen with a sense of humor enjoy big mischief.

My grandfather was not "a County Dublin squireen": his ancestral property was in the town of Carlow (I inherited it at his son's death, and, having restored it to solvency, gave it to the District Council). He lived at Oughterard in Galway as a country gentleman, fishing, shooting, and doing his own carpentering and boat building as a very handy amateur.

Page 37. Aunt Ellen, though humpbacked, was not a midget.

St Bride's was not near by Synge Street. It was away in the slums, and has been long since demolished, as only the Catholic poor lived there. Its registers recorded my christening; but whether they were burnt in the Four Courts during the civil war, or are preserved in the library of Trinity College, reports vary.

Page 39. No city clerk could afford to live in Synge Street. Most of the householders were, like my father, merchants, not opulent, but of superior social pretensions to shopkeepers.

Bushy Park was and is a country house, quite outside

Dublin city at Rathfarnham, though the postal address is Terenure.

Page 41. My father never laughed when he was drunk. On the occasion when he mistook the wall of the Dalkey cottage for the gate and made a concertina of his tall hat by butting at it, the laughter came from his son and his brother-in-law.

Page 42. Miss Caroline Hill must have taught me a good deal which I have no recollection of learning, and for many adult years believed I knew by nature. One day I suddenly realized that this was nonsense; and, Miss Hill being long dead, I became a subscriber to the Governess's Benevolent Institution. I cannot remember learning to read; but I do remember a wet afternoon on the quays when I sheltered with my father in a portico plastered with posters, and, being small enough to be carried in his arms, electrified the crowd by reading all the posters aloud.

Page 43. There was no "profusion of musical instruments lying about." When I broke my father's trombone to find out what was inside it only the piano was left.

Page 44. This is a tissue of blunders. Lee was a mesmeric conductor, and had collected an amateur orchestra, eked out occasionally by a soloist from a military band. But the notion that orchestral rehearsals could fit into our house is absurd. They took place in the Antient Concert Rooms in Brunswick Street: the rehearsals in the Banner room and performances in the Concert Room. At the rehearsals in our house the accompaniments were played on the piano. The neighbors never complained: the music was too good; and there was no "din."

When his brother died Lee lived in Harrington Street with an old housekeeper, reputedly a terror. She was got rid of somehow; and the arrangement by which our households combined at No. 1 Hatch Street, followed.

Except that Uncle William played the ophicleide in Lee's band there was no musical contact with the Shaw relatives, who could all vamp popular tunes on various instruments by ear, but were quite uncultivated classically.

Cousin Emily, who played the cello, was Aunt Emily, wife of the rector of St Bride's, and my father's sister. She disliked my mother, and never came to Synge Street. One day my mother paid her a visit and overheard her exclaim "That bitch!" when she was announced. The incident ended their acquaintance.

Page 45. There is an omission on this page. Nearly all Lee's best singers were Roman Catholics; and our intercourse with them rooted out of my mind the notion that Catholics are inferior people, not to be associated with, and all predestined to eternal damnation. I still like them better and respect them above the Protestant snobocracy.

The Dalkey cottage on Torca Hill overlooked both Dublin and Killiney bays, and was quite outside and high above the little town of Dalkey. Killiney strand was not shingly: it was sand from end to end. Torca Cottage now bears a handsome plaque commemorating my residence there. It was unveiled in January 1948, and gratified me immensely.

Page 46. At that time tuberculosis was called decline or consumption, and was not considered infectious. My sister Agnes caught it from a housemaid, and after a rapid decline died in the Isle of Wight, not in a sanatorium.

Our house in the Fulham Road was in a *cul de sac* nearly opposite the West Brompton Post Office. It was then called Victoria Grove and is now rechristened Netherton Grove. Number 13 has been demolished and replaced by big buildings, like all the semi-detached villas on the east side; but the last villa on the opposite side is a replica of 13.

Page 47. I never argued with my father nor asked him why? why? why?. A a child, I asked him what? what? what? as all children ask their parents. Under this pressure he told me many things that he did not know, improvising his answers on the spur of the moment, and, as I found out later on, quite correctly. Such is the magic of parentage.

Page 49. I had never read the 39 Articles, and did not know of their existence. As to Mary Wollstonecraft, I had never heard of her. Paine had been held up to me as a drunken staymaker without a redeeming trait. Voltaire and Rousseau, I was taught, were blasphemers whose deathbeds were made frightful by their certainty of going to hell. It was then part of the education of a gentleman to convince him that the three most religious men in Europe had been impious villains, and were roasting in blazing brimstone to all eternity. Shelley cured me of all that. I read him, prose and verse, from beginning to end. This took place at the end of my teens.

Page 51. I was not "conscious of my own talents." I was disabled for many years by imagining that everybody knew as much as I knew and could do everything rather better. My bane has always been diffidence. I was wise enough to be overwhelmed by my ignorance, and innocent enough to imagine that I was the only ignoramus in the world. I was a coward until Marx made a Communist of me and gave me a faith. When it turned out later on that I was a born Shakespearean genius I flattered myself that Nature, alias Providence, alias The Life Force, had given me in my boyhood an excessive regard for self-preservation lest I should throw away my genius in some pugnacious adventure. Anyhow when I was a boy I was a coward, and bitterly ashamed of it.

Ayot Saint Lawrence,
1947-8

15

ORIGIN OF CORNO DI BASSETTO

I OBJECTED TO THE
Star's fuss about its fiftieth birthday; for it reminded me that
I was over eighty. Its birth seems to me an event of the day
before yesterday.

It is now respectably settled in the Fleet-Street precinct;
but its birthplace was in the wilds of Farringdon Market in
a street called Stonecutter Street, and in a building constructed
for the purpose. It seemed then to be an exceptionally high
one, as it had a square courtyard presenting an appalling
precipice in case of fire to the occupants of the top storey.

The arrangement was that Tay Pay (Edmund Yates's
name for the late Irish T. P. O'Connor, M.P., Star founder
and editor) was to live there; but Mrs T. P., when she saw
the precipice, demurred. So they affixed to her bedroom
window a canvas tube by way of fire escape. She insisted on
trying it before the vendor's men left the premises; but as
nobody in London, then or now, has the faintest notion of
how to use the articles they sell, she was not told that she
must use her elbows as brakes.

Mrs T. P. just got into the tube and let go.

She shot down like lightning down a conductor, coming out at the foot, which the men were holding up, in a parabolic curve which ended against the opposite wall. Anybody but Mrs T. P. would have been killed; but she, without turning a hair, only told the dismayed holders what she thought of their fire escape.

Mrs T. P. found her voice in a Star feature of which T. P. was very proud. Edmund Yates had made his sixpenny weekly paper, The World, very popular in the West End by columns of society gossip headed What The World Says. Such a thing in a halfpenny paper devoted to "putting two lumps of sugar in the washerwoman's teacup instead of one" (T. P.'s adaptation of Swift's famous two grains of wheat instead of one) was unheard of; but T. P. rightly maintained that washerwomen are as keen on society gossip as duchesses. He let Mrs T. P. loose in a column headed Mainly About People. She opened it with "Lady Colin Campbell is the only woman in London who has her feet manicured."

She was a very attractive American lady, was Mrs T. P.; but T. P. was unable to rise to the height of his good fortune. The marriage was not a success. The top flat with its fire escape was abandoned; and the two parted, leaving Mainly About People less unintentionally amusing.

T. P.'s editorship was rather like his marriage. He started the paper with great vigor and all possible *éclat;* but when it came to carrying it on he was hampered by the fact that his political outlook had become fixed in Ireland in the eighteen-sixties, and was thenceforth a stopped clock. Though I have no reason to believe that he disliked any individual Englishman except Joseph Chamberlain, whom he called Judas, he, like a good graduate from Galway College, hated the English in the lump.

When the Fabian Society captured the first London County Council and plunged it into municipal Socialism disguised as Progressivism, T. P. did not know where he was. When his first lieutenant, H. W. Massingham, then known as The Boy, and their adjutant Ernest Parke, tried to educate him Progressively, John Morley remonstrated with all his Front Bench authority, and frightened T. P. back into his quaint combination of British Palmerstonian diplomacy and Free Trade Liberalism with Irish Fenianism dressed up as Home Rule.

Presently twenty letters arrived at Stonecutter Street fiercely protesting against his backsliding, producing the effect of a tremendous rising of the whole country; and though Massingham assured his chief that all the letters were written by me (which was near enough to the truth, as I had given the word to twenty Fabians to let fly) T. P. was none the less impressed. That is the nature of editors.

I had joined The Star staff as a leader writer on Massingham's recommendation on the second day of its existence; for, on the first, such strict orders were given to the doorkeeper to exclude all questionable characters that he refused to admit any member of the literary profession. T. P. dared not print any of my leaders, as the paper was starting as a Liberal organ, and I was a constitutional but strenuous Socialist, my sole object in joining The Star being to foist Fabian municipal Socialism on it.

But London rose so promptly to the Fabian program that the first County Council election was fought and won on it, but not before old Gladstonian Liberals, bewildered by what was to them a most dangerous heresy, had forced me to retire from the editorial staff, and beg for the humble job of contributing a weekly column about music. As it seemed to T. P. that I could do no harm there, he assented with a gasp of relief. Hence the weekly column signed Corno di Bassetto. T. P. attached no importance to it; for the ignorance of daily newspaper editors of the fine arts at that time is now hardly credible, as their nightly duties made it impossible for them to attend theatres or concerts. Any incomprehensible jargon could be palmed on them as art criticism. The wireless has made an end of this.

It very soon appeared that I had used the word music in Plato's sense; for I wrote about everything I pleased: first, by taking care that Corno di Bassetto should always be amusing: second, by using a knowledge of music and of political economy which nobody suspected me of possessing, to provide a solid substratum of genuine criticism for the levities and irrelevances of Bassetto. Finally, far from being superseded I superseded T. P., whose Palmerstonian articles were as hopelessly out of date as Bassetto's column was ahead of it.

TO FRANK HARRIS ON SEX IN BIOGRAPHY

FIRST, O SEX-OBSESSED
Biographer, get it into your mind that you can learn nothing about your biographies from their sex histories. The sex relation is not a personal relation. It can be irresistibly desired and rapturously consummated between persons who could not endure one another for a day in any other relation. If I were to tell you every such adventure I have enjoyed you would be none the wiser as to the sort of man I am. You would know only what you already know: that I am a human being. If you have any doubts as to my normal virility, dismiss them from your mind. I was not impotent; I was not sterile; I was not homosexual; and I was extremely susceptible, though not promiscuously.

Also I was entirely free from the neurosis (as I class it) of Original Sin. I never associated sexual intercourse with delinquency, nor had any scruples or remorses or misgivings of conscience about it. Of course I had scruples, and effectively inhibitive ones too, about getting women "into trouble" or cuckolding my friends; and I held chastity to be a passion just as I hold intellect to be a passion; but St Paul's case was to me always pathological. Sexual experience seemed a natural appetite, and its satisfaction a completion of human experience necessary for fully qualified authorship. I was not attracted by virgins as such. I preferred fully matured women who knew what they were doing.

You were amazed and incredulous when I told you that my first adventure did not occur until I was 29. But it would be a prodigious mistake to take that as the date of the beginning of my sexual life. Do not misunderstand this: I had been perfectly continent except for the involuntary incontinences of dreamland, which were very unfrequent. But as between Oscar Wilde who gave 16 as the age at which sex begins, and Rousseau who declared that his blood boiled with it from his birth, my personal experience confirms Rousseau and confutes Wilde. Just as I cannot remember any time when I could not read and write, I cannot remember any time when I did not exercise my imagination in daydreams about women.

All young people should be votaries of the Uranian Venus to keep them chaste: that is why Art is vitally important. I was steeped in romantic opera from my childhood. I knew all the pictures and antique Greek statues in the National Gallery of Ireland. I read Byron and everything of romantic fiction I could lay my hands on. Dumas *père* made French history like an opera by Meyerbeer for me. From our cottage

MY SISTER ELINOR AGNES

MRS. JENNY PATTERSON

My Lady Friend in 1885

on Dalkey Hill I surveyed an enchanting panorama of sea, sky, and mountain. I was overfed on honey dew. The Uranian Venus was bountiful.

The difficulty about the Uranian Venus is that though she can save us from premature debaucheries, and enable us to prolong our physical virginity long after budding adolescence, she can also sterilize us by giving us imaginary amours on the plains of heaven so magical that they spoil us for real women and real men. We may become celibate through a surfeit of beauty and an excess of voluptuousness. We may end as ascetics, saints, old bachelors or old maids, because, like Heine, we cannot ravish the Venus of Milo or be ravished by the Hermes of Praxiteles. Our love poems, like Shelley's Epipsychidion, only irritate *terre à terre* sensual men and women, who know at once that we are in love with our own vision and only pretending that they are something they are not and neither desire nor hope to be.

Now you know how I lived, a continent virgin, but an incorrigible philanderer, until I was 29, running away when the handkerchief was thrown to me; for I wanted to love, but not to be appropriated and lose my boundless Uranian liberty. During the 14 years before my marriage at 43 there was always some lady in the case; and I tried all the experiments and learned what there was to be learnt from them. The ladies were unpaid; for I had no spare money: I earned only enough to keep me on a second floor, taking the rest out not in money but in freedom to preach Socialism. Prostitutes, who often accosted me, never attracted me. As soon as I could afford to dress presentably, I became accustomed to women falling in love with me. I did not pursue women: I was pursued by them.

Here again do not jump to conclusions. All my pursuers did not want sexual intercourse. Some were happily married, and appreciated our understanding that sex was barred. They wanted Sunday husbands, and plenty of them. Some were prepared to buy friendship with pleasure, having learnt from a varied experience that men are made that way. Some were enchantresses, quite unbearable as housemates. No two cases were alike. William Morris's dictum "they all taste alike" was not, as Longfellow puts it, "spoken to the soul."

I was never duped by sex as a basis for permanent relations, nor dreamt of marriage in connection with it. I put everything else before it, and never refused or broke an engagement to speak on Socialism to pass a gallant evening. I valued sexual experience because of its power of producing a celestial flood of emotion and exaltation which, however momentary, gave me a sample of the ecstasy that may one day be the normal condition of conscious intellectual activity.

Not until I was past 40 did I earn enough to marry without seeming to marry for money, nor my wife at the same age without suspicion of being driven by sex starvation. As man and wife we found a new relation in which sex had no part. It ended the old gallantries, flirtations, and philanderings for both of us. Even of these it was the ones that were never

178

consummated that left the longest and kindliest memories.

Do not forget that all marriages are different, and that marriages between young people, followed by parentage, must not be lumped in with childless partnerships between middleaged people who have passed the age at which the bride can safely bear a first child.

So now, no romance. Above all, no pornography.

1930

17

HOW FRANK OUGHT TO HAVE DONE IT

THE LATE FRANK HAR-
*ris was a distinguished figure in literary London in the last
decade of the nineteenth century. As editor of The Fortnightly Review and subsequently and especially of The Saturday Review he surrounded himself with a galaxy of brilliant
writers chosen with uncommon judgment and courage, myself
among them. His own works included short stories of the
kind then made fashionable by De Maupassant, a biography
of Oscar Wilde, a book on Shakespear, a scandalously candid
autobiography (later on), and a series of notably trenchant
and pungent Contemporary Portraits.*

*In one of these, purporting to be a portrait of me, he was
neither trenchant nor pungent; for in writing it he had been
embarrassed and disabled by a sense of obligation to me
because I had remained loyal to our old connection through
a period in which he was neither popular nor prosperous, and
had to take refuge finally in exile. The result was a piously*

*grateful eulogy which made me laugh; so I took up my pen
and sent him the following example of how he ought to have
portrayed me.*

*Harris published it in his last volume of Contemporary
Portraits; but I cannot believe he ever read it. He knew next
to nothing of my career after The Saturday Review episode.
When he was dying an American publisher commissioned
him to write a biography of me; and his needs obliged him
to make a desperate attempt to fulfil this task. But his inven-
tions and conjectures were so wide of the mark, that to enable
them to be published after his death I had to rewrite his book
myself on matters of fact, thus doing seriously what in the
following lines I had done as a jeu d'esprit.*

*I have taken this opportunity to add some sentences which
could only have been written by Harris's ghost, as they mention circumstances which occurred after his death*

*Dramatizing myself from an objective point of view (the
method natural to me) enabled me to say things I could not
gracefully have said from my own subjective angle: but it
obliges me to add Errors and Self-Delusions Excepted.*

Before attempting to add Bernard Shaw to my collection
of Contemporary Portraits, I find it necessary to secure myself
in advance by the fullest admission of his extraordinary
virtues. Without any cavilling over trifles I declare at once
that Shaw is the just man made perfect. I admit that in all his
controversies, with me or anyone else, Shaw is, always has

been, and always will be, right. I perceive that the common habit of abusing him is an ignorant and silly habit, and that the pretence of not taking him seriously is the ridiculous cover for an ignominious retreat from an encounter with him. If there is any other admission I can make, any other testimonial I can give, I am ready to give it and apologize for having omitted it. If it will help matters to say that Shaw is the greatest man that ever lived, I shall not hesitate for a moment. All the cases against him break down when they are probed to the bottom. All his prophecies come true. All his fantastic creations come to life within a generation. I have an uneasy sense that even now I am not doing him justice: that I am ungrateful, disloyal, disparaging. I can only repeat that if there is anything I have left out, all that is necessary is to call my attention to the oversight and it shall be remedied. If I cannot say that Shaw touches nothing that he does not adorn, I can at least testify that he touches nothing that he does not dust and polish and put back in its place much more carefully than the last man who handled it.

I will tell some anecdotes of Shaw. Oscar Wilde said of him "He has not an enemy in the world; and none of his friends like him."

Once, at a public dinner given by the Stage Society, Shaw had to propose the health of the dramatic critics; and Max Beerbohm had to reply. Before the speaking began Max came to Shaw and said "You are going to say, aren't you, that you are a critic yourself?" "I dont know what I am going to say" said Shaw; "but I daresay I could bring that in." "Promise me that you will" said Max: "I want to make a point about it." "Anything to oblige you" said Shaw; and he did. Max began his speech thus: "I was once at a school where the master used always to say 'Remember, boys, I am one of yourselves.'" A roar of laughter saved Max the trouble of pointing the moral.

Robert Lynd said of Shaw's Common Sense About the War that though nobody could take any reasonable exception to it, yet, from the moment it appeared, the war was spoken of and written about as a war between the Allies on the one hand, and, on the other, Germany, Austria, Turkey, and Bernard Shaw.

When Shaw contested a seat at the London County Council election as a Progressive, after six years' hard Progressive drudgery on a Borough Council, with the advantage of being one of the inventors of municipal Progressivism, not only was he defeated by the defection of all but the irreducible minimum of Liberals and temperance reformers (Shaw is a teetotaller), but the leading Progressive papers openly exulted in his defeat as a most blessed deliverance. The only other people who voted for him were those who had never voted before. This was proved by an increase in the poll at the next election, when the 'adored actor George Alexander was the victorious candidate.

These are the things that happen to him in his most popular moments, when he is in no way breasting and opposing the

MY FAVORITE IMAGE OF HIM. COST ME 23 SHILLINGS

G.B.S., LAURA KNIGHT R.A. AND SIGMUND STROBL

Together in Malvern in 1932

current of public opinion. When, as often happens, he has to take his chance of being lynched for telling some unpalatable truth, numbers of persons who have never before dared to betray any hostility to him believe that they have him "on the run" at last, and vent on him a bitterness and violence which must have been rankling in them for years.

The result is that hardly anyone who has not met Shaw thinks of him otherwise than as a man of disagreeable appearance, harsh manners, and insufferable personality. He knows this, and says "I always astonish strangers by my amiability, because, as no human being could possibly be so disagreeable as they expect me to be, I have only to be commonly civil to seem quite charming."

No truthful contemporary portrait can ignore either this extraordinary power of exciting furious hostility, or the entire absence of any obvious ground for it. It has been said that Shaw irritates people by always standing on his head, and calling black white and white black. But only simpletons either offer or accept this account. Men do not win a reputation like Shaw's by perversity and tomfoolery. What is really puzzling is that Shaw irritates us intensely by standing on his feet and telling us that black is black and white white, whilst we please ourselves by professing what everyone knows to be false.

There is something maddening in being forced to agree with a man against whom your whole soul protests. It is not that he expresses your own view more accurately than you urself could. But you cannot bear your inmost convictions to be shared by a man whose nature you hold to be monstrous and subversive. It is as if a man had offered to walk a bit of the way with you because you were going in the direction of his home, and you knew that home to be the bottomless pit.

As a matter of fact there is nothing in Shaw's political and social program, not even his insistence on basic equality of income and its dissociation from every kind of personal industry or virtue, at which a thinker of adequate modern equipment need turn a hair. He is a perfectly safe man on a committee of any sort: a man of tact and circumspection who kept the Fabian Society, of which he was a leader for twenty-seven years, free from the quarrels that broke up all the other Socialist organizations.

Yet the monstrosity is there; for Shaw works at politics in the spirit of one helping a lame dog over a stile which he believes to be insurmountable. "Every man over forty is a scoundrel!" he proclaimed when he was himself over forty. He makes no secret of his conviction that the problems raised by modern multitudinous civilization are beyond our political capacity and may never be solved by us. He attaches little value to mere experience, holding that it is expectation of life and not recollection of it that determines conduct. He reminds us repeatedly that as Evolution is still creative Man may have to be scrapped as a Yahoo, and replaced by some new and higher creation, just as man himself was created to supply the deficiencies of the lower animals.

It is impossible to take offence at this, because Shaw is as merciless to himself as to us. He does not kick us overboard and remain proudly on the quarter deck himself. With the utmost good-humor he clasps us affectionately round the waist and jumps overboard with us, and that too, not into a majestic Atlantic where we might perish tragically, but into a sea of ridicule amid shrieks of derisive laughter. And this intolerable trick is played on us at the most unexpected and inopportune moments. "No man" said Sir Henry Norman "knows how to butter a moral slide better than Shaw." Shaw's championship thus becomes more dreaded than the most spiteful attacks of others. During the first Ibsen boom in London he proposed to help an American actress in an Ibsen enterprise by interviewing her. To his astonishment the lady told him with passionate earnestness that if he wrote a word about her she would shoot him. "You may not believe here in England that such things are possible" she said; "but in America we think differently; and I will do it: I have the pistol ready." "General Gabler's pistol" was Shaw's unruffled comment; but he saw how intensely the lady shrank from being handled by him in print; and the interview was not written. Some of his best friends confess that until they were used to him quite friendly letters from him would sometimes move them to furious outbursts of profanity at his expense. He tells a story of a phrenologist with whom he got into conversation at a vegetarian restaurant in his early days. This man presently accused Shaw of being "a septic," meaning a sceptic. "Why?" said Shaw. "Have I no bump of veneration?" "Bump!" shouted the phrenologist. "It's a hole." If Shaw's manners were offensive one could at least punch his head; but his pity for your inadequacy and his own is so kindly, so covered by an unexceptionable observance of the perfect republican respect to which you are entitled, that you are utterly helpless: there is nothing to complain of, nothing to lay hold of, no excuse for snatching up the carving knife and driving it into his vitals.

I, Frank Harris, was editing The Fortnightly Review when I first met Shaw about an article. He had an engaging air of being more interested in me than in the article. Not to be mock modest, I suppose I *was* more interesting than the article; and I was naturally not disposed to quarrel with Shaw for thinking so, and shewing it. He has the art of getting on intimate and easy terms very quickly; and at the end of five minutes I found myself explaining to him how I had upset my health by boyishly allowing myself to be spurred into a burst of speed on the river in an outrigger, and overstraining myself. He gave his mind to my misfortune as sympathetically as my doctor, and asked me some questions as to how much care I was taking of myself. One of the questions was "Do you drink?" I was equal to the occasion, and did not turn a hair as I assured him that a diagnosis of delirium tremens could not be sustained; but I could not help becoming suddenly conscious that I expected from men an assump-

tion that I am not a drunkard, and that I was face to face
with a man who made no such assumption. His question was
too like one of those asked in Butler's Erewhon to be entirely
agreeable to human frailty. In Shaw's play Captain Brass-
bound's Conversion, the captain introduces his lieutenant
with the words (or to this effect) "This is the greatest scoundrel, liar, thief, and rapscallion on the west coast." On which
the lieutenant says "Look here, Captain: if you want to be
modest, be modest on your own account, not on mine." The
fact that Shaw *is* modest on his own account, and gives himself away much more freely than his good manners allow him
to give away his friends, does not really make the transaction
any more agreeable to its victims: it only robs them of their
revenge, and compels them to pay tribute to his amiability
when they are furiously annoyed with him.

It is difficult to class a man who gives himself away even
to the point of making himself ridiculous as vain. But all
Shaw's friends agree that he is laughably vain. Yet here again
he confuses our judgment by playing up to it with the most
hyperbolical swank about his intellect. He declares that he
does so because people like it. He says, quite truly, that they
love Cyrano, and hate "the modest cough of the minor poet."
Those who praise his books to his face are dumbfounded
by the enthusiasm with which he joins in his own praise, and
need all their presence of mind to avoid being provoked into
withdrawing some seventy-five per cent. or so of their eulo-
gies. Such playacting makes it difficult to say how much real

vanity or modesty underlies it all. He himself denies that he is conceited. "No man can be" he says "if, like me, he has spent his life trying to play the piano accurately, and never succeeded for a single bar." I ask him to give me a list of his virtues, his excellences, his achievements, so that I may not do him the injustice of omitting any. He replies "It is unnecessary: they are all in the shop window."

Shaw plays the part of the modest man only in his relations with the arts which are the great rivals of literature. He has never claimed to be "better than Shakespear," though he does claim to be his successor. The much quoted heading to one of his prefaces has a note of interrogation after it; and the question is dismissed by himself with the remark that as Shakespear in drama, like Mozart in opera, and Michael Angelo in fresco, reached the summit of his art, nobody can be better than Shakespear, though anybody may now have things to say that Shakespear did not say, and outlooks on life and character which were not open to him.

Nevertheless I am convinced that Shaw is as willing to have his plays compared with Shakespear's as Turner was to have his pictures hung beside Claude's. Yet when he was invited to a dinner in Paris in honor of Rodin, he wrote that he had the honor of being one of Rodin's models, and was sure of a place in the biographical dictionaries a thousand years hence as "Shaw, Bernard: subject of a bust by Rodin: otherwise unknown." He struck the same note when, finding that Rodin, though an infallible connoisseur in sculpture, had no books in his collection except the commonest kind of commercial presentation volumes, he presented him with a Kelmscott Chaucer, and wrote in it

I have seen two masters at work: Morris who made this book:
The other Rodin the Great, who fashioned my head in clay.
I give the book to Rodin, scrawling my name in a nook
Of the shrine their works shall hallow when mine are dust by
    the way.

In the same vein is the inscription he proposed for a pedestal to Lady Kennet's statue of him, now in the Bournemouth Municipal Gallery.

WEEP NOT FOR OLD GEORGE BERNARD: HE IS DEAD
AND ALL HIS FRIENDS EXCLAIM "A DAMNED GOOD JOB!"
THOUGH RANKING GEORGE'S CELEBRATED HEAD
HIGH IN THE MORE UNCOMMON SORTS OF NOB

LONG AT ITS IMAGE KATHLEEN'S HAND HAD PLIED
WHEN THE LORD SAID "NOT THUS GREAT WORK BEGAT IS.
COPY NO MORE: YOUR SPIRIT BE YOUR GUIDE:
CARVE HIM SUB SPECIE AETERNITATIS

SO WHEN HIS WORKS SHALL ALL FORGOTTEN BE
YET SHALL HE SHARE YOUR IMMORTALITY"

Later on The Evening News asked him to write his own epitaph. In response he drew a weed-overgrown tombstone, and on it the lines

191

HIC JACET

BERNARD SHAW

Who the devil was he?

Now I confess I am not convinced by this evidence of modesty. I am not sure that it is not rather the final artistic touch to Shaw's swank. For what was the origin of the Rodin bust? Rodin knew nothing about Shaw, and at first refused to undertake the commission. Mrs Shaw thereupon wrote to Rodin pleading that she wished to have a memorial of her husband, and that her husband declared that any man, who, being a contemporary of Rodin, would have his bust made by anyone else, would pillory himself to all posterity as an ignoramus. Rodin, finding that he had to deal with a man who knew his value, weakened in his refusal. Mrs Shaw then ascertained from Rilke, the Austrian poet, then acting as Rodin's secretary, what his usual fee was for a bust. The money (£1,000) was immediately lodged to Rodin's credit on the understanding that he was to be under no obligation whatever in respect of it, and might make the bust or not make it, begin it or leave it off at his pleasure: in short, treat the payment as a contribution to the endowment of his work in general and remain completely master of the situation. The result, of course, was that Rodin sent for Shaw to come to Paris at once; installed him and his wife as daily guests at his Meudon villa; worked steadily at the bust every day for a

CLOSE-UP OF SIGMUND STROBL WITH ME ON THE BALCONY OF THE MALVERN HOTEL IN 1932

IN MY FORTIES

IN MY NINETIES

month until it was finished; and went beyond his bargain in giving the sitter casts of it.

Here we have the diplomatic Shaw, the master of blarney, and the penetrating art critic; and not for a moment do I suggest that there was the slightest insincerity in his proceedings. Had there been, Rodin would not have been taken in. But was there no vanity in it? Would so busy a man as Shaw have left his work and gone to Paris to pose like a professional model for a whole month if he had not thought his bust as important as the busts of Plato which are now treasures of the museums which possess them?

Shaw is an incorrigible and continuous actor, using his skill as deliberately in his social life as in his professional work in the production of his own plays. He does not deny this. "G.B.S." he says "is not a real person: he is a legend created by myself: a pose, a reputation. The real Shaw is not a bit like him." Now this is exactly what all his acquaintances say of the Rodin bust, that it is not a bit like him. But Shaw maintains that it is the only portrait that tells the truth about him. When Rodin was beginning the work in his studio, Mrs Shaw complained to him that all the artists and caricaturists, and even the photographers, aimed at producing the sort of suburban Mephistopheles they imagined Shaw to be, without ever taking the trouble to look at him. Rodin replied "I know nothing about Mr Shaw's reputation; but what is there I will give you." Shaw declares that he was as good as his word. When Paul Troubetskoy saw the bust he declared that there was no life in the eyes; and in three hours frenzied work he produced his first bust of Shaw, now in America. As a *tour de force* it is magnificent; but it is Mephistopheles, not suburban, but aristocratic. Shaw liked the bust, and liked Troubetskoy; but his wife would have none of it, nor of the curious portrait by Neville Lytton, suggested by Granville-Barker's remark that Velasquez's portrait of Pope Innocent was an excellent portrait of Shaw. Lytton accordingly painted Shaw in the costume and attitude of Innocent; but though the picture shews what Shaw would be like in the papal chair, Pope Bernard will never be identified by any antiquary with the subject of the Rodin bust.

Augustus John's three portraits of Shaw are even less reconcilable with the Rodin. John has projected all Shaw's public strength and assurance at their fullest intensity, indeed at more than lifesize. "There is the great Shaw" says the sitter when he shews his friends the picture. But when he points to the Rodin, he says "Just as I am, without one plea." De Smet's portrait is that of a quiet delicate elderly gentleman: Shaw likes its resemblance to his father. The statuette by Lady Scott is friendly and literal: the half length statue by Lady Kennet of the Dene (the same lady) is a companion to that of Shakespear in Stratford church. Sigmund Strobl's bust ranks with those by Rodin and Troubetskoy. Troubetskoy finally modelled Shaw at full length, lifesize, in his platform pose as an orator. This fine bronze has come to rest in the National Gallery of Ireland, which possesses also his portrait by John Collier, prosaic, but lifelike enough to have been mistaken by Mrs Shaw for Shaw himself in Collier's studio. Mrs Shaw was fastidious about portraits of her husband. Of Laura Knight's she said to G.B.S. "Laura has given you her own singleminded sincerity; but you are always acting." On seeing a photograph of Epstein's famous bust (the last) she said "If that thing enters this house I leave it"; and it never did. Shaw admired its workmanship but acknowledged it only as representing some aboriginal ancestor of his. Davidson's bust is a spirited but hasty sketch.

No wonder H. G. Wells complained that he could not move a step without being outfaced by an effigy of Shaw. Modest Shaw may be; but he has sat for memorials of himself by the greatest masters of his time. Can such modesty be justified until he has been dead for at least five hundred years?

Shaw is the greatest pedant alive. Dickens's man who ate crumpets on principle could not hold a candle to him in this respect. Descriptive reporters have said that Shaw wears a flannel shirt. He never wore a flannel shirt in his life. He does not wear a shirt at all, because it is wrong to swaddle one's middle with a double thickness of material: therefore he wears some head-to-foot under-garment unknown to shirt-makers. The flannel fable arose because, at a time when it was socially impossible for a professional man to appear in public in London without a white starched collar, he maintained that no educated eye could endure the color contrast of ironed starch against European flesh tones, and that only a very black and brilliant negro should wear such a collar. He therefore obtained and wore grey collars. Now that the fashion is changed, he wears collars of various colors; but the dye is always chosen to carry out a theory that the best color effect is that of two shades of the same color. His jacket is of the smartest West End tailoring; but it is unlined, on principle. He formerly addressed his letters high up in the left hand corner of the envelope. A mere affectation of singularity, you say. Not at all: he would talk to you for an hour on the beauty of the system of page margins established by the medieval scribes and adopted by William Morris, and on its leaving space for the postman's thumb. When the postman complained that the postmark obliterated the address Shaw returned to the normal practice.

He justifies his refusal to use apostrophes and inverted commas in printing his books on the ground that they spoil the appearance of the page, declaring that the Bible would never have attained its supreme position in literature if it had been disfigured with such unsightly signs. He is interested in phonetics and systems of shorthand; and it is to his pedantic articulation that he owes his popularity as a public speaker in the largest halls, as every word is heard with exasperating distinctness. He advocates a combination of the metric system with the duodecimal by inserting two new digits into our numeration, thus: eight, nine, dec, elf, ten, and eighteen, nineteen, decteen, elfteen, twenty, and so forth. He likes machines as a child likes toys, and once very nearly bought a cash register without having the slightest use for it. When he was on the verge of sixty he yielded to the fascination of a motor bicycle, and rode it away from the factory for seventy-seven miles, at the end of which, just outside his own door, he took a corner too fast and was left sprawling. He has been accused of being one of the band of devoted lunatics who bathe in the Serpentine throughout the year, rain or shine; but this is an invention, founded on his practice of swimming in the bathing pool of the Royal Automobile Club every morning before breakfast, winter and summer, his alleged reason being that as an Irishman he dislikes washing himself, but cannot do without the stimulus of a plunge into cold water. He is, as all the world knows, a vegetarian, valuing health highly but declaring that men who are any good trade on their stocks of health to the utmost limit, and therefore live on the verge of a breakdown. All really busy men, he holds, should go to bed for eighteen months every forty years to recuperate. I could easily fill another page with his fads; but I forbear.

Shaw's gallantries are for the most part non-existent. He says, with some truth, that no man who has any real work in the world has time or money for a pursuit so long and expensive as the pursuit of women. He may possibly have started the protest against the expensiveness and the exactions of beautiful women which is the main theme of Harley Granville-Barker's Waste and The Madras House. Nobody knows his history in this respect, as he is far too correct a person to kiss and tell. To all appearances he is a model husband; and in the various political movements in which his youth was passed there was no scandal about him. Yet a popular anecdote describes a well known actor manager as saying one day at rehearsal to an actress of distinguished beauty "Let us give Shaw a beefsteak and put some red blood into him." "For heaven's sake dont" exclaimed the actress: "he is bad enough as it is; but if you give him meat no woman in London will be safe."

Anyhow, Shaw's teaching is much more interesting than his personal adventures, if he ever had any. That teaching is unquestionably in very strong reaction against what he has called Nineteenth Century Amorism. He is not one of your suburban Love is Enough fanatics. He maintains that chastity is so powerful an instinct that its denial and starvation on the scale on which the opposite impulse has been starved and denied would wreck any civilization. He insists that intellect is a passion, and that the modern notion that passion means only sex is as crude and barbarous as the ploughman's idea that art is simply bawdiness. He points out that art can flourish splendidly when sex is absolutely barred, as it was, for example, in the Victorian literature which produced Dickens. He compares Giulio Romano, a shameless pornographer, pupil of Raphael and brilliant draughtsman, with Raphael himself, who was so sensitive that though he never painted a draped figure without first drawing it in the nude, he always paid the Blessed Virgin the quaint tribute of a *caleçon* in his studies of her, and contrived to decorate the villa of a voluptuary with the story of Cupid and Psyche without either shrinking from the uttermost frankness or losing his dignity and innocence. Shaw contends that when art passed from Raphael to Giulio it fell into an abyss, and became not only disgusting but dull.

The eternal triangle of the Paris stage he rejects as proving adultery to be the dryest of subjects. He wrote Plays for Puritans to shew how independent he was of it. He demands scornfully whether genuine virility can be satisfied with stories and pictures, and declares that the fleshly school in art is the consolation of the impotent.

Yet there are passages in his plays which urge that imaginary love plays an important part in civilized life. A handsome hero says to a man who is jealous of him "Do not waste your jealousy on me: the imaginary rival is the dangerous one." In Getting Married, the lady who refuses to marry because she cannot endure masculine untidiness and the smell of tobacco, hints that her imagination provides her with a series of adventures which beggar reality. Shaw says that the thousand and three conquests of Don Juan consist of two or three squalid intrigues and a thousand imaginative fictions. He says that every attempt to realize such fictions is a failure; and it may be added that nobody but a man who had tried could have written the third act of Man and Superman. In the final act of that play, too, the scene in which the hero revolts from marriage and struggles against it without any hope of escape, is a poignantly sincere utterance which must have come from personal experience. Shakespear in treating the same theme through the character of Benedick might conceivably have been making fun of somebody else; but Tanner, with all his extravagances, is first hand: Shaw would probably not deny it and would not be believed if he did.

Shaw's anti-Shakespear campaign under my Saturday Review editorship was all the more unexpected because I was one of the few London editors to whom Shakespear was more than a name. I was saturated with Shakespear. That I should be the editor of an attack on Shakespear of unheard-of ferocity was the one thing I should have declared confidently could never possibly occur to me. What made the adventure odder was, first, that Shaw, who delivered the attack, was as full of Shakespear as I: second, that though we were both scandalized by the sacrilege we were committing, neither of us could honestly alter a word in one of the articles. They were outrageous; but there was nothing to withdraw, nothing to soften, nothing that could be modified without bringing down the whole critical edifice.

The explanation is simple enough. Shaw's first shot at Shakespear was fired in 1894. Ibsen's first broadside on England caught the London theatre between wind and water in 1889. Shaw had written his Quintessence of Ibsenism in the meantime, and was judging everything on and off the stage by the standard set up by the terrible Norwegian. Many lesser men fell short of that standard; but Shakespear was the most conspicuous victim. "It is useless to talk of Shakespear's depth now" said Shaw: "there is nothing left but his music. Even the famous delineation of character by Molière-Shakespear-Scott-Dumas-*père* is only a trick of mimicry. Our Bard is knocked out of time: there is not a feature left on his face. Hamlet is a spineless effigy beside Peer Gynt, Imogen a doll beside Nora Helmer, Othello a convention of Italian opera beside Julian." And it was quite true. Only in the Sonnets could we find Shakespear getting to the depth at which Ibsen worked.

Shaw was full not only of Ibsen, but of Wagner, of Beethoven, of Goethe, and, curiously, of John Bunyan. The English way of being great by flashes: Shakespear's way, Ruskin's way, Chesterton's way, without ever following the inspiration up on which William Morris put his finger when he said that Ruskin could say the most splendid things and forget them five minutes after, could not disguise its incoherence from an Irishman. "The Irish" he says "with all their detestable characteristics, are at least grown up. They think systematically: they dont stop in the middle of a game of golf to admire a grandeur of thought as if it were a sunset, and then turn back to their game as the really serious business of their life." His native pride in being Irish persists in spite of his whole adult career in England and his preference for English and Scottish friends.

It will be noticed that my portrait of Shaw is both more and less intimate than any other I have penned. More, because Shaw tells the whole world all that there is to be told about himself. Less, because I have never sat on a committee with him; and that is the only way to see much of him. Shaw is not really a social man. He never goes anywhere unless he has business there. He pays no calls. Once he was induced by Maurice Baring to go to a bachelor's party of the usual British type, with grown men throwing lumps of bread at one another, telling smutty stories, and conscientiously striving to behave like rowdy undergraduates. "Gentlemen," said Shaw, with deadly contempt for their efforts, "we shall enjoy ourselves very much if only you will not try to be convivial." On their persisting he got up and left. He complains that only in the presence of women will men behave decently.

After lunching at the Savile Club on his arrival in London he resolved that he would never be a literary man nor consort with such. "I might have spent my life sitting watching these fellows taking in each other's washing and learning no more of the world than a tic in a typewriter if I had been fool enough" he says. I tried to cure him of this by inviting him to my Saturday Review lunches at the Café Royal; but it was no use. He came a few times, being sincerely interested in the Café, in the waiters, in the prices, in the cookery: in short, in the economics of the place; but he concluded that Harold Frederic and I ate too many steaks, and that it was a waste of money to pay Café Royal prices for his own plateful of macaroni, which he could obtain elsewhere for tenpence. The fact that I paid for it made no difference: he objected to a waste of my money just as much as of his.

I have sometimes wished that other people were equally considerate; but Shaw's consideration amounts to an interference with one's private affairs that is all the more infuriating because its benevolence and sagacity makes it impossible to resent it. All attempts to draw him into disinterested social intercourse are futile. To see as much of Shaw as I could easily see of any other man of letters in London, I should have had to join his endless committees. Our relations as contributor and editor were useless for social purposes: he came to the office only when we were in some legal difficulty, mostly to demonstrate with admirable lucidity that we had not a leg to stand on. He is accessible to everybody; but the net result is that nobody really knows him.

There is a cutting edge to Shaw that everybody dreads. He has in an extreme degree the mercurial mind that recognizes the inevitable instantly and faces it and adapts itself to it accordingly. Now there is hardly anything in the world so unbearable as a man who will not cry at least a little over spilt milk, nor allow us a few moments murmuring before we admit that it is spilt and done for. Few of us realize how much we soften our losses by veiling them in an atmosphere of sympathies, regrets, condolences, and caressing little pretences that are none the less sweet because they are only anesthetics. Shaw neither gives nor takes such quarter. An Indian prince's favorite wife, when banqueting with him, caught fire and was burnt to ashes before she could be extinguished. The prince took in the situation at once and faced it. "Sweep up your missus" he said to his weeping staff "and bring in the roast pheasant." That prince was an oriental Shaw.

Once at Westminster Bridge underground station, Shaw slipped at the top of the stairs, and shot down the whole flight on his back, to the concern of the bystanders. But when he rose without the least surprise and walked on as if that were his usual way of descending a flight of steps they burst into an irresistible laugh. Whether it is a missed train, or a death among his nearest and dearest, he shews this inhuman self-possession. No one has accused him of being a bad son: his relations with his mother were apparently as perfect as anything of the kind could be; but when she was cremated, Granville-Barker, whom he had chosen to accompany him as the sole other mourner, could say nothing to him but "Shaw: you certainly are a merry soul." Shaw fancied that his mother was looking over his shoulder and sharing the fun of watching two men dressed like cooks picking scraps of metal from her ashes. He is fond of saying that what bereaved people need is a little comic relief, and that this is why funerals are so farcical.

In many ways this mercurial gift serves Shaw's turn very well. He knows much sooner and better than most people when he is in danger and when out of it; and this gives him an appearance of courage when he is really running no risk. He has the same advantage in his sense of the value of money, knowing when it is worth spending and when it is worth keeping; and here again he often appears generous when he is driving a very good bargain. When we stand amazed at his boldness and liberality, it is doubtful how far he is capable of facing a real danger or making a real sacrifice. He is genuinely free from envy; but how can he be envious when he can pity every other man for not being George Bernard Shaw? The late Cecil Chesterton has left it on record that when he, as a young nobody, met the already famous Shaw, he was received on terms of the frankest boyish equality. This shews only that Shaw makes no mistakes about men and manners. All that can be predicted of him is unexpectedness.

And so, with all his engaging manners and social adroitness, Shaw often seems one who does not care what he says, nor what others feel. It explains why "he has not an enemy in the world; and none of his friends like him." His Cæsar's "He who has never hoped can never despair" is imposing; but who can feel sure that its inspiration is not infernal rather than divine? Compare it with the piously hackneyed "This is the true joy in life, the being used for a purpose recognized by yourself as a mighty one; the being thoroughly worn out before you are thrown on the scrap heap; the being a force of Nature instead of a feverish little selfish clod of ailments and grievances complaining that the world will not devote itself to making you happy." There is no smell of brimstone about this; but ask any of Shaw's fans which of the two quotations is the more Shavian.

I shall not attempt to carry the portrait any further. Shaw is almost a hopeless subject, because there is nothing interesting to be said about him that he has not already said about himself. All that he has left for me to deal with is something that has escaped not only his biographers but himself. Neither he nor they have ever attempted to explain Wilde's epigram. He is violently resented and hated as well as admired and liked. Pinero signed a friendly private letter to him "with admiration and detestation."

I have tried to depict a consistent character (and Shaw's character is almost mechanically consistent) that can produce such contrary effects. Nobody has yet tried to do this: his defenders have ignored the dislike: his assailants have denied his qualities and invented faults which do not exist. I have made no attempt to sit in judgment nor play the chivalrous friend. I have sketched the man's lines as they appear; and though the resultant figure is free from deformity, yet he can give us all a shudder by saying "Imagine a world inhabited exclusively by Bernard Shaws!" This is only a trick; for a world of anybody would be unbearable. But there is something in it for all that; and what that something is I leave you to discover, not understanding it myself.

24th May 1919

206

ENVOY

Of these reminiscences and memoranda I must now make an end, as there must be an end to everything. I have tried, as I promised, not to plague my readers with details common to myself and ninetynine and a half per cent. of the human race; but I have included matter that, though not peculiar to myself, may be instructive to beginners in my various professions or to historians of my period. I have added nothing about my married life in the twentieth century; for it has been so public that any biographer can ascertain more of it than I can myself remember. Whether the result is readable or not I am in doubt; for at my age (over 90) I cannot be sure that my sayings and writings are not the senile drivellings of a garrulous and too old man.

However, enough of it was written years ago to embolden me to let it take its chance, such as it is. I will not even say Hail and Farewell; for I have still enough kick left to make fresh outbursts possible.